EVERYDAY HABITS FOR TRANS- FORMING SYSTEMS

T0356244

EVERYDAY HABITS FOR TRANS- FORMING SYSTEMS

The Catalytic Power of
Radical Engagement

ADAM KAHANE

A Reos Partners Publication

Berrett–Koehler Publishers, Inc.

Berrett-Koehler Publishers, Inc.
1333 Broadway, Suite P100
Oakland, CA 94612-1921
Tel: (510) 817-2277
Fax: (510) 817-2278
bkconnection.com

ORDERING INFORMATION
Quantity sales. Special discounts are available on quantity purchases by corporations, associations, and others. For details, please go to bkconnection.com to see our bulk discounts or contact bookorders@bkpub.com for more information.
Individual sales. Berrett-Koehler publications are available through most bookstores. They can also be ordered directly from Berrett-Koehler: Tel: (800) 929-2929; Fax: (802) 864-7626; bkconnection.com.
Orders for college textbook / course adoption use. Please contact Berrett-Koehler: Tel: (800) 929-2929; Fax: (802) 864-7626.

Distributed to the US trade and internationally by Penguin Random House Publisher Services. The authorized representative in the EU for product safety and compliance is EU Compliance Partner, Pärnu mnt. 139b-14, 11317 Tallinn, Estonia, www.eucompliancepartner.com, +372 5368 65 02

Berrett-Koehler and the BK logo are registered trademarks of Berrett-Koehler Publishers, Inc.

Printed in the United States of America

Berrett-Koehler books are printed on long-lasting acid-free paper. When it is available, we choose paper that has been manufactured by environmentally responsible processes. These may include using trees grown in sustainable forests, incorporating recycled paper, minimizing chlorine in bleaching, or recycling the energy produced at the paper mill.

Library of Congress Cataloging-in-Publication Data

Names: Kahane, Adam, author.
Title: Everyday habits for transforming systems : the catalytic power of radical engagement / Adam Kahane.
Description: First edition. | Oakland, CA : Berrett-Koehler Publishers, Inc., [2025] | Includes bibliographical references and index.
Identifiers: LCCN 2024044539 (print) | LCCN 2024044540 (ebook) | ISBN 9781523006861 (paperback) | ISBN 9781523006878 (pdf) | ISBN 9781523006885 (epub)
Subjects: LCSH: Social change. | Social action.
Classification: LCC HM831 .K34 2025 (print) | LCC HM831 (ebook) | DDC 303.48/4 -- dc23/eng/20241221
LC record available at https://lccn.loc.gov/2024044539
LC ebook record available at https://lccn.loc.gov/2024044540

First Edition
32 31 30 29 28 27 26 25   10 9 8 7 6 5 4 3 2 1

Book production: Susan Geraghty
Cover design: Ashley Ingram and Siobhan Wilkinson
Cover and interior illustrations by Siobhan Wilkinson

For my fellow journeyers

CONTENTS

PREFACE

This book is for everyone who wants to create a better world.

This is for you.

For the activist fighting hard for solutions to climate problems.

For the parent painstakingly organizing a coalition so that children can be educated for the future rather than the past.

For the entrepreneur implementing a bold business plan for a world-changing product that requires a new supply network.

For the nonprofit manager frustrated with running emergency relief programs, searching for a way to prevent the emergencies.

For the philanthropist promoting alternative economic models.

For the facilitator striving to resolve a deeply rooted conflict.

For the consultant whose clients can accomplish their ambitious missions only by partnering with unlikely others.

For the public servant running a multi-organization health program that supports access not only to doctors and medicines but also to decent food, jobs, housing, and care.

For the civic leader who knows that genuine democracy requires not only well-run elections but also social cohesion and the regulation of campaign financing and social media.

For the local politician battling crosscurrents, committed to creating a community where everybody really belongs.

This is for you.

For all of you who want to contribute to creating a world

with more connection, agency, and justice, and less fragmentation, oppression, and inequity.

For those of you who already see that all these things—we as individuals and collectives; our culture, technology, organizations, markets, and politics; our Earth—are part of interconnected, interdependent, interrelated *systems*, and therefore that the only way to make the changes you want is to change these systems.

And for those who simply sense these things and are looking for words to describe this sense and for actions to make a difference.

This is for you.

This is for us.

TRANSFORMING SYSTEMS

A system is a set of elements (people, other beings, machines, institutions, rules, etc.) that is structured, intentionally or otherwise, so that it achieves a purpose or produces a characteristic pattern of behavior. We live in systems and we cocreate them. They enable some of us to feed, clothe, house, transport, heal, entertain, protect, and govern ourselves, and impede others of us from doing so. They work for some of us and against others of us.

Regardless of our degree of awareness of these systems, much of the time we don't think that we need to change them or are able to do so.

- We might not even be aware that we are part of systems: we are focused just on what is happening immediately around us, and think that this could change if only somebody—the president, a boss, a spouse, ourselves—would change.

- We might be aware of being part of systems, but think that they're working well enough.

- We might think that systems are not working well, but that there is nothing we can do to change them.

- We might think that systems are not working well, but that all we can realistically do is tweak them so that they work a little less badly.

So we concentrate on looking after ourselves and the people we're close to, and living as well as we can with things as they are. But sometimes we know we must and can contribute to changing systems—indeed to transforming them fundamentally so that they work better for more people.

This book is for everyone—activist, parent, entrepreneur, manager, philanthropist, facilitator, consultant, public servant, civic leader, politician, and/or simply a concerned and committed person—who wants to transform systems.

EVERYDAY HABITS

These transformations don't just require long-term strategies or daring initiatives. They also require a particular way of being, thinking, relating, and acting, day in and day out—a set of habits to disrupt ourselves and the systems we are part of.

This book explains how such individual everyday actions, which any of us can take, can contribute to collective long-term transformation. It explains how attending to changing these small things that we can control enables us to contribute to changing larger things that we cannot control.

This book matters now because so many of us can see that many of our systems are in crisis—they're working terribly and urgently need to be transformed—but don't know what we can do to contribute to this transformation. Moreover, we can see that these crises (and the attendant fear, anger, polarization, and violence) are creating both breakdowns and breakthroughs— but we don't know what we can do to attenuate the former and amplify the latter.

For more than three decades, I have worked alongside hundreds of people who are creating systemic breakthroughs: people with and without formal authority, in all kinds of organizations, from all fields and sectors, at all levels and scales, all around the world. I've been impressed by their ability to make a difference, but haven't understood what exactly it is they do that enables them to make such an impact.

To write this book, I talked with many of these people about their experiences, searching for the simple day-to-day practices that any of us, no matter what our position or power, can employ to contribute to transformation. This book reports what I've learned from these people: seven everyday habits for transforming systems.

EVERYDAY HABITS FOR TRANS-FORMING SYSTEMS

TRANSFORMING SYSTEMS REQUIRES RADICAL ENGAGEMENT

How can we contribute to transforming the systems we are part of? I'd spent thirty years doing this, so thought I knew the answer to this question. But three thirty-minute conversations, on September 16, September 28, and October 7, 2021, revealed that I didn't.

DISCOVERING THAT I DIDN'T KNOW

My colleagues and I help teams from across a given system—be it an organization, sector, community, or country—work together to transform that system. We facilitate processes through which civil society, government, and business leaders collaborate, over months and years, to implement solutions to complex problems related to food, education, health, energy, climate, security, justice, peace, and democracy. I had just published my fifth book about this work, *Facilitating Breakthrough: How to Remove Obstacles, Bridge Differences, and Move Forward Together*, and had the idea of publicizing it by conducting brief live online interviews with famous "facilitators."

So I reached out to three people I knew who had played significant roles in important transformations: Trevor Manuel, a South African activist and later politician involved in the extraordinary transition from apartheid to democracy; Christiana Figueres, a Costa Rican diplomat and later United Nations official who led the negotiation of the landmark Paris Agreement on climate change; and Juan Manuel Santos, a Colombian journalist and later president who was awarded the Nobel Peace Prize for ending his country's long civil war.[1]

I was nervous because I had never conducted public interviews like these, but confident that I knew my stuff.

The interviews didn't go as I'd expected.

I thought we'd talk about things I was expert in, but we didn't. I discovered that although I did know something about systems transformation, it was as a sometime supporter and observer from the outside. I didn't know much about what it takes to do this work, day in and day out, from the inside. I realized that there is something vitally important in the everyday work of transforming systems that I and others—not only top leaders like these three but all of us at all levels who want to contribute to creating a better world—need to understand.

This realization led me on a journey that has produced, after many twists and turns, the book you are reading now, and the way of understanding systems transformation that I will summarize in this introduction.

AN EMBLEMATIC EXAMPLE OF
SYSTEMS TRANSFORMATION

When scholars make lists of historic systems transformations, they always put near the top the transition in South Africa from brutal settler colonialism and racist apartheid (a system that worked much better for White than Black people) to liberal, nonracial democracy. Many people, in many places, over many decades, through many battles, employing many strategies—mass movements, boycott and divestment, parliamentary opposition, diplomatic pressure, armed resistance, moral argumentation—together effected this change.

(I am starting this book with the extraordinary South African example because it illustrates many key characteristics of systems transformation and because it provides the background to my first interview, with Trevor Manuel, which I recount in the next section. If you already know this background, you can skip ahead now.)

The South African story is a powerful tale of the transformation of a system away from fragmentation, oppression, and inequity, toward connection (across racial, ethnic, and national divides), agency (of every person, Black as well as White), and justice (overcoming colonial and apartheid injustices). But it is not a fairy tale in which everything changed and everyone lived happily ever after. Some of the fundamental structures of South Africa have changed: there are new institutions, infrastructures, and ideas, and everyone now has equal political and legal rights. And some of the fundamental structures have not changed: many of the old institutions, infrastructures, and ideas are still there, and the degree of social and economic inequality are still the highest in the world.

Real-world transformation always includes victories, defeats, surprises, compromises, reversals, and unfinished business. "Out of the crooked timber of humanity," philosopher Immanuel Kant said, "no straight thing was ever made."[2] Transformation can be wonderful and joyful—but, as you will hear me say many times in this book, it is never easy or straightforward.

AN EXEMPLARY SYSTEMS TRANSFORMER

One of the people central to the South African transition was Trevor Manuel, whom I first met in September 1991 when I was thirty years old and he was thirty-five. Journalist Alex Perry describes how Manuel had begun his activism:

> Under the apartheid racial-classification system, he was considered "colored," or mixed race, and thus confined to a home in the Cape Flats, the hot, treeless townships between breezy Table Mountain and leafy Stellenbosch. As a 5-year-old, he witnessed apartheid's bite when his classmates were divided by color. "Suddenly half the kids in my class at school were no longer there," he says. "And so politics came to me." In the 1970s, Manuel gravitated towards Steve Biko's Black Consciousness movement. But in 1979, determined to become "a revolutionary with a big beard and a big gun," he traveled to Botswana to join the African National Congress guerrillas in exile. To his disappointment, the ANC sent him back to work in Cape Town. He quickly became a key figure in the city's opposition and by 1985 he was in jail. Regular detentions followed. During one release, Manuel, who had married, met his toddler son for the first time.[3]

In 1991, after the African National Congress (ANC) was legalized, Manuel was appointed head of its Department of Economic Planning; in 1994, when the ANC won the first national democratic election, he entered parliament and served twenty years in the cabinet of President Nelson Mandela and his successors (thirteen years as the country's first Black Minister of Finance, overseeing a period of sustained economic growth); and after he retired from politics in 2014, he became the chair of the country's biggest insurance company. So for decades he has been a prominent and popular player in the transformation of South Africa.

I got to know Manuel when I was facilitating the first of four weekend workshops at the small Mont Fleur (Flower Mountain) conference center in the beautiful wine country east of Cape Town. In these meetings, he and twenty-seven other leaders from across South African society—Black and White, women and men, from the opposition and the establishment, left and right—energetically hammered out a set of four scenarios of possible futures for their country, as a way to figure out how to get to democracy.[4] They chose to participate in the meetings because they knew that, with the release of Mandela from prison and the legalization of the opposition parties, they had a once-in-a-lifetime opportunity to shape the future.

From across their diverse positions, this team of leaders wrestled with the basic questions that are crucial for any transformation: What in this system is working and not, and for whom? What must and can be changed? The conclusion of their intense arguments was that if South Africans could avoid several particular political and economic risks (failing to negotiate a settlement, constraining the capacity of a new democratic government, ignoring fiscal constraints), then they could start to build a democracy. And South Africans did avoid these risks and did, in April 1994, start to build a democracy.

The Mont Fleur project contributed to the transformation of South Africa, in part by helping Manuel and others deepen both their understanding of and their relationships across this fractured system. Beyond this it came to exemplify, within the country and beyond, the wonderful possibility of diverse people working together to transform a system so that it works better for more people.

During the time I was facilitating the Mont Fleur project, I was working for Shell, the international energy company, as leader of the London head-office team that studied global political, economic, social, technological, and environmental futures. The project organizers had asked Shell to lend me to the project because of my methodological expertise. The team noticed the incongruity of a Canadian corporate expert facilitating a group of mostly leftist South African leaders; Manuel joked about this when he introduced me to the team as "a representative of International Capital." But they could tell that my intention was to support them in making their own assessment of possible futures for the country rather than to impose my own. Howard Gabriels, a former official of the socialist National Union of Mineworkers, later told me: "When we first met you, we couldn't believe that anyone could be so naïve: we were certain that you were trying to manipulate us. But when we realized that you actually didn't know anything, we decided to trust you."

Working with this team was my first experience of engaging with people who were trying not just to do well within a given system but to transform it, and it upended my career and life. By the end of the project, I had resigned from Shell, emigrated to

South Africa, and taken up a vocation of supporting such system transformers.

Many of the members of the Mont Fleur team had devoted their lives to "the struggle" against apartheid. Some had been in prison or in exile or underground; all had done difficult and conflictual work. Among the members of this remarkable group, Manuel struck me as especially charismatic, moving constantly around the room, engaging in friendly banter with everyone, encouraging them to work together across their differences. I connected with him personally because Dorothy Boesak, the project coordinator whom I met during the workshops (and later married), knew him as "a nice young man," and it was Manuel who mischievously announced to the team that she and I had become romantically involved.

At that time and over the decades that followed, Manuel was at the center of the country's debates about policies to enable Black people to move from the margins of the economy to the center. He was generous but measured in his assessment of the impact of Mont Fleur on the decisions of the ANC government. When two researchers from the Massachusetts Institute of Technology interviewed him in 2000, he reflected: "It's not a straight line. It meanders through, but there's a fair amount in all of it going back to Mont Fleur that we were able draw through. I could close my eyes and give the scenarios to you just like *this*. I've internalized them and if you have internalized certain things then you probably carry it for life."[5]

Manuel knows firsthand what it takes to transform systems. He summarized the whole period of transformation and what it required of the people involved: "You see, there was the degree of flux. That was a real strength. There was no paradigm, there was no precedent, there was nothing. We had to carve it, and so perhaps we were more willing to listen. . . . What you need to equip people with is a set of skills which allows them to ask questions: to actively engage in their everyday lives. If you can crack that, you will have cracked it."[6] He understands that when people are working with a system that is in flux and ripe for transformation, listening and asking questions are vitally important.

THE EVERYDAY WORK OF TRANSFORMING SYSTEMS

When I contacted Manuel in 2021 to ask to interview him, he accepted graciously. But after a warm start, our interaction became testy as I kept interrupting him to try to get him to affirm the model of transformative facilitation that I had written about in *Facilitating Breakthrough*, and he kept trying to get across to me his very different understanding.

He explained what he had done to build consensus in support of the transition in terms of days and days of tough meetings with many diverse groups of people, working to find a way forward together:

> What we needed to do was to persuade a diversity of institutions and views. In one morning I would be with a group of business leaders in an affluent area, and in the afternoon at the university campus with some very radical students, and in the evening in a very poor community.
>
> We needed to persuade everybody that the struggle needed to find a conclusion. Bear in mind that there were very deep and gaping scars then, still: many of us had been to prison, many had been in exile, many had lost friends and associates. All that we and I could do

was to try and persuade people that we had one shot at this, and that persuasion created the basis for the absence of significant resistance.

That was kind of the day job; the night job was to work with other groupings in the African National Congress to try and define what the shape and form of South Africa would be.

Then he described his later work as minister of finance, also in terms of finding a way forward that made sense to many groups with different perspectives and interests:

The minister of finance gets this one big shot a year, which is when you table the budget proposals. I would speak to four hundred members of Parliament who have to vote these proposals into law. And you're also speaking to traders sitting on trading floors around the world, who are judging what you're doing. Then you have a constituency of people—and I've always taken the view of my mother, who was a pensioner (sometimes she would be in the gallery at Parliament and other times with others at home)—whom I needed to satisfy about the decisions I was taking. Also trade unions, who have a vested interest in this as well, and they have voice. So whilst we had the ability to present the budget in highfalutin economic language, it was also important that we communicated with people.

So you take all of these constituents and you need to be conscious of them, and your strength and the consensus that you can arrive at is through speaking to all of those.

Then he told me a story that I thought was off topic:

> A few years ago, I was in discussion with an academic
> who said that he was in awe of my ability to engage and
> arrive at conclusions and not feel threatened by other
> people. So we had a long discussion about this, and he
> said to me that in his life as an academic from the time
> he gone to graduate school, he was on his own, either
> in the library or at a desk working on his dissertation.
> And then when he graduated with a master's degree, he
> needed to do a PhD, and that was even longer, but it was
> entirely isolated, and the ethos of that kind of academic
> is to produce for yourself.
>
> But we in the anti-apartheid movement came from
> an environment where it was not competitive: our
> thoughts needed to be developed collaboratively so that
> we could get other people to come along.

Only later did I grasp that this story was very much *on* topic—
that Manuel was trying to explain that transformation doesn't
happen the way I thought it did.

As soon as the live interview was over, I got messages from
Dorothy and my colleagues telling me that in pressing Manuel
to agree with my thinking about what it takes to effect transformation I had been a terrible interviewer and shouldn't quit my
day job.

I was mortified, and also perplexed.

I was used to thinking about systems transformation in
terms of exceptional, compressed, high-level, elegant, heroic,
macro efforts. But Manuel had spoken in terms of everyday,
extended, on-the-ground, messy, collective, micro conversations. I realized that systems transformation looks different to

a peripheral observer and facilitator like me as compared to a central protagonist like him.

This is when I started to wonder about everyday habits for transforming systems, and to realize that I needed to write this book—not only for others but for myself.

METAPHORS FOR TRANSFORMING SYSTEMS: CARVING, WEAVING, SAILING

In the weeks after this conversation with Manuel, I talked with Christiana Figueres and then Juan Manuel Santos. (I recount these latter two interviews later in this book.) I came away from this set of encounters energized and intrigued.

Through the high-profile roles these three leaders have played over decades—activist, politician, businessperson, diplomat, negotiator, warrior, thought leader, elder—they have contributed, as significantly as any people I know of, to transforming big, important systems. (These transformations were, as always, incomplete and imperfect, and all three have their critics.) Even in their most powerful roles, however, they were not able to force the systems to be the way they wanted, so they had to engage with others, including their opponents, to shape the way the systems have continued to evolve.

But I wasn't yet able to make out from their stories a pattern in what they had been doing, day-to-day, that had enabled them to achieve what they had and that might be instructive for other people working on systems transformation in their own contexts.

I began to think back about what I had seen over the years of working with system transformers: not about the macro processes that I had been paying attention to but about these individuals' micro actions, which I had been ignoring.

I saw a clue in the metaphors that my three interviewees had used. Manuel spoke about "carving," which I understood to mean working with our hands, creatively, to bring into being something new—carving is not the same as assembling. Figueres spoke about "weaving," meaning bringing together diverse contributions to make something jointly owned and beautiful—not the same as manufacturing. And Santos spoke about "sailing," meaning working with forces beyond our control to get where we want to go—not the same as steamrolling.

These three images all hinted that transforming a system involves a craft of working intentionally and intimately with the natural material of the system (including the people who are part of it), not to impose on it but to bring out its potential.

To make sense of the everyday actions of systems transformers, I realized that I first needed to answer a basic question: How are systems transformed? And I started on this by answering the opposite question: How are systems *not* transformed?

HOW SYSTEMS ARE NOT TRANSFORMED

A system tends to keep doing what it's doing; that's what it's for. It can be transformed so that it does something different if and only if enough people want to transform it, have the power to transform it, understand how to do so, and are willing and able to act on that understanding.

A system is not transformed if most people think that what it's doing is fine—that as far as they're concerned, it doesn't need to be transformed.

A system is not transformed if most people think it's doing terribly but that there's nothing they can realistically do to change it—that they have no option other than to live with the system as it is or adjust it so that it works a little less terribly.

And a system is not transformed if most people don't under-stand that it's a system—a set of elements that is structured such that it keeps doing what it does—and so don't understand how to change what it's doing.

HOW SYSTEMS ARE TRANSFORMED

The first thing we need to understand is that we live in systems that we have created and can recreate. Journalist Naomi Klein says,

> We should stop treating a great many human-made systems—like monarchies and supreme courts and borders and billionaires—as immutable and unchange-able. Because everything some humans created can be changed by other humans. And if our present systems threaten life to its very core, and they do, then they must be changed.[7]

A system can sometimes be changed by a few people with power forcing it to change. But such transformations are usually degenerative: they produce more fragmentation, oppression, and inequity—and therefore usually don't last. This book is about how to transform systems generatively and sustainably: to produce more connection, agency, and justice.

Systems are transformed generatively not by one person or team taking one big transformative action but rather by many people taking many small actions, separately and together, for many reasons. So this book is addressed not to people who are in control of a system (few of us ever are) but to all of us who are part of a system and want to contribute to changing it.

Many aspects of many systems are working terribly and

need to be transformed, but many other aspects are working well and so need to be protected and maintained. Systems are therefore transformed generatively not through general or black-and-white actions ("Change everything!") but rather through specific and nuanced actions that address what, why, and when to transform, by who and for whom, and how.

Systems include some people and exclude others. They benefit and empower some people more than others, whether these elites are constructed along the lines of caste, class, color, rank, race, ethnicity, education, ability, gender, sexual orientation, political affiliation, country of origin, or other characteristics. Generative systems transformation that increases justice by changing who gets what can be wonderful and joyful, but the process is never serene, straightforward, or safe; it is always disruptive and difficult and often dangerous. (And remember: the status quo is also difficult and dangerous for those people whom the system is currently not benefiting.)

In summary, generative systems transformation is not routine, controlled, predictable, simple, linear, quick, calm, or easy; it is contextual, responsive, surprising, complex, emergent, cumulative, rough, and challenging—like the dynamics of life and death on an African savanna among elands, lions, vultures, trees, dung beetles, and others.

THERE IS A CRACK IN EVERYTHING

So how can systems be transformed generatively? Poet Leonard Cohen offers another metaphorical clue in his song "Anthem" when he says that illumination and possibility arise through "cracks."

Systems might appear to be solid, but they aren't. Cracks

A generative system

are places in a system where things are shifting—breakdowns and bright spots—and creating openings for something new to emerge, like cracks in the earth out of which plants can grow. (I'll be developing this point further in the chapter on Habit 4.)

We transform systems generatively by feeling our way forward—step by step, sensitively, imperfectly, through trial and error—to discover, open up, and move through cracks. Feeling our way forward means working intentionally, fully present, and hands-on with a system that is in the process of changing—we're not just forcing change.

Contrary to what people will try to tell you or sell you, there is no universal recipe for transforming systems, so this book doesn't provide one. There is no one right thing—be it politics or community or entrepreneurialism or change management or self-development—that everyone must do. There is no silver bullet, master plan, sure bet, shortcut, or easy victory. And there is no guarantee that what we do will have the impact we intend.

The best we can do, then, is to pay attention and make a next move that we think will enable us to advance, a move that fits with the particularities of our capacity and context: who we are, in relationship with whom, with what influence, where, and when. Then we step back, observe our impact, and make another move.

Entrepreneur Charly Clermont uses the analogy of prospecting for gold to describe his decades of efforts to create a better Haiti. He told me,

> Transforming a system requires transforming its structure, which requires looking for the places in the system at which we can act: leverage points or cracks. It's like a

group of us are looking for gold. We know what we are looking for, but every day we have to decide where we're going to go and what we're going to do. Every day we do and then we talk: What did you find? This is how we learn and build a community of people who can make a difference.

We transform systems through working with cracks.

THE CATALYTIC POWER OF RADICAL ENGAGEMENT

How do we discover a next move that enables us to contribute to transformation? When I looked at the approaches used by Manuel, Figueres, Santos, Clermont, and others, I couldn't see a simple answer. I ended up staring at long lists: everyone has their particular approach to making their way forward in their particular context.

When I stepped back from these lists and squinted, however, I could see one simple, ordinary, practical pattern.

Manuel and the others had told me stories of the day-in, day-out processes of meeting, listening, talking, arguing, convincing, cajoling, compromising, and working together. Manuel spoke of doing this, before the 1994 election, with business leaders, radical students, poor communities, groups within the ANC, and other political parties, and later as minister of finance with members of parliament, traders, pensioners, trade union representatives, and constituents. In his interview in 2000 he had referred to such processes as follows: "We had to carve it, and so perhaps we were more willing to listen," and this had required equipping people "to ask questions: to actively engage in their everyday lives." This is the fully engaged, hands-on, conflictual, and collaborative approach to transformation that neither I nor the ivory tower academic in Manuel's "off-topic" story had been able to recognize.

Finally I was able to see what Manuel had been pointing me toward: the pattern that had been in front of my eyes for thirty years that I had missed.

The way to transform a system generatively is through working with cracks. We do this not by sledgehammering the system but by *engaging* in give-and-take with it, meaning "taking part in; pledging oneself to; holding fast; entering into conflict with." And not by engaging superficially in a way that keeps the system as it is (as in "I have a dinner engagement"), but by doing so *radically* (from the Latin *radix* or root), meaning "going to the root(s); affecting the foundation; naturally inherent, essential, fundamental."[8] (In this book I am using this primary and original meaning of the word radical, not its secondary meaning of "extreme.")

The core message of this book is that the foundational way of being, relating, and acting required to transform systems generatively is *radical engagement*:

- Radical engagement refers to the day-in, day-out practice of intentionally and consciously colliding, connecting, communicating, confronting, competing, and collaborating with people from different parts and levels of the system, at the cracks, working together with them to transform that system. Radical engagement is the simple—but not easy—activity of meeting others fully.

- Radical engagement with a system doesn't mean participating in that system distractedly, resigned, knowing it all, hierarchically, at arm's length, with arms crossed, superficially, impatiently, saying take it or leave it. It means taking part in it alertly, with hope and curiosity, horizontally, leaning forward, hands-on, digging deep, persisting, and above all reciprocally and relationally.

• Radical engagement is a way of creating more connection, agency, and justice through interacting with others, exercising our own agency and inviting theirs, justly. It is a way of being and acting that reduces fragmentation, oppression, and inequity. It is an antidote to the poisons of othering and authoritarianism that are sweeping the world.

• Radical engagement consists of small actions—moves, nudges, probes—that can create big impacts. It is a powerful catalyst of systems transformation. It is the fundamental practice underneath all strategies and tactics for transforming systems generatively.

A system—be it a family, an organization, a sector, or a nation—is transformed generatively through the actions of different people in different positions in the system doing different things over time. Anyone in any position can engage radically with others around them to work the cracks within their reach and thereby, one step at a time, through trial and error, contribute to effecting transformation.

THE NEED FOR TRANSFORMATIONAL HABITS

Generative systems transformation is a long-term process that requires sustained radical engagement. It's not a "one and done" job, so a spasm of engagement, no matter how fundamental or radical, usually doesn't make much of a difference. To be able to contribute substantially, we therefore need to develop our capacity to engage radically not just as an exceptional, occasional action but as an everyday practice or habit. These habits are essential for all of us—not just a special few in highfalutin professional roles—who want to contribute to transforming systems in our daily lives, day in and day out.

Developing everyday habits isn't about welding on new extraordinary capacities, but about unblocking and releasing capacities that, deep down, most of us already have. We do this by stretching, as we would physical stretching: by practicing these actions regularly, with perseverance and discipline; going beyond our comfort zones, sometimes painfully; and taking rests, thereby over time expanding our range of comfortable motion. We have to stretch to become more able to engage radically and to contribute to generative systems transformation.

THE SEVEN HABITS OF RADICAL ENGAGEMENT

I've written this book to clarify and share the everyday practices of radical engagement. My three interviews in 2021 showed me how crucial these practices are, even though I did not yet understand them.

To write it I've engaged with accomplished systems transformation practitioners, talking about their experiences in a wide variety of contexts: climate, democracy, education, energy, food, health, housing, land, peace, security, and self-determination; locally, nationally, and globally; from across the Americas, Europe, Africa, Asia, and Australasia. These practitioners work in government, business, research, nonprofit, and community-based organizations, but most of them—like most of you—also approach the work of systems transformation as concerned and committed citizens.

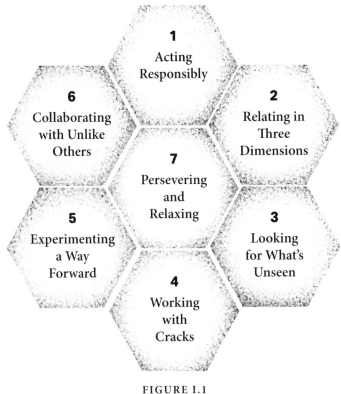

FIGURE I.1

Seven habits of radical engagement

Through this inquiry, I have gradually been able to identify seven habits of radical engagement—and to discern how these radical habits involve consciously stretching beyond the comfortable conventional habits that many of us unconsciously fall into (see figure I.1).

HABIT 1: Acting Responsibly—not just doing what is expected of us, nor just whatever we like

HABIT 2: Relating in Three Dimensions (engaging with others as fellow actors, parties, and kin)—not just in the one or two dimensions that we're most comfortable with

HABIT 3: Looking for What's Unseen—not just seeing what we always see

HABIT 4: Working with Cracks—not just ignoring or shying away from them

HABIT 5: Experimenting a Way Forward—not just doing what's familiar or safe

HABIT 6: Collaborating with Unlike Others—not just with people who are like us and whom we like

HABIT 7: Persevering and Resting—not just sprinting for a short while, nor pushing on until we burn out

These habits also aren't new. Many people have written books to help professionals use one or another of the habits—learning, experimenting, collaborating, and so on—to act effectively within current systems. The purpose of this book, however, is different: to help anyone use these habits to act effectively to *transform* systems.

As a set, these habits fit together into an integrated, holistic way of being and acting. The stories I tell in the coming chapters are of diverse practitioners who each practice many of these habits (not only the habit described in the chapter in which I narrate their story). When, overall, our habitual everyday engagement is constrained, cautious, and comfortable, then we are able only to engage superficially and to contribute to keeping things as they are. But when, like these practitioners, we stretch our habitual everyday engagement beyond our comfort zone in some or all of these seven ways, then we become more able to engage beneath the surface and thereby contribute to generative transformation.

The system transformers I have spoken with have, collectively, revealed a vision of what being radically engaged looks like. Writing this book has helped me get clearer about what I have been doing (even if I wasn't thinking about my actions in these terms) and what I need to do to contribute to transforming systems: which habits I already do quite well (2, 3, 5, 7) and which I need to learn to do better (1, 4, 6). This vision has nudged me to make different everyday choices: to stretch beyond my cocooned comfort zone and into the less comfortable but more effective zone of radical engagement. As I wrote it, every chapter challenged my way of being, relating, and acting.

The purpose of this book is not to enable a few of us to employ radical engagement perfectly but to enable many of us to employ radical engagement better.

Systems transformation practitioner Fyodor Ovchinnikov, referring to the challenges his colleagues face in Russia, explained why these habits and stretches really matter:

> If you are in a place that is really crying out for transformation—not just like, "Hmm, maybe I should transform something because that's what I like to do"—then these habits help you stay sane and on purpose. Habits shape strategy. In complex systems, you can't have a good plan but you can have a good presence, and these habits design our being. A lot of times habits are imposed by the system and include ones like, don't say anything, don't trust anyone, or don't look outside of your tunnel vision. When we become more conscious about our habits, they can actually be lifesavers, by enabling us to get unstuck and build cohesion for collective action.

These habits enable all of us to contribute to transforming the systems we are part of.

WHAT THIS BOOK OFFERS

This book explains how any of us, whatever our position and power, can contribute to the long-term, collective, extraordinary, often-overwhelming work of systems transformation through practicing a set of seven daily, individual, ordinary, doable habits. The book isn't saying that if we can just heroically change ourselves, then systems will change. It's saying that if we practice this particular engaged way of being, relating, and acting, then we'll be able, together with others, to more effectively contribute to changing systems. And changing systems to become more connected, just, and agential in turn enables all of us to more readily change ourselves. Individual and collective change are mutually reinforcing.

The next seven chapters spell out the seven habits. Habit 1, Acting Responsibly, is a foundational way of being, relating, and acting through which we take responsibility for the roles in the system that we are currently playing and need to play. By exercising Habit 2, Relating in Three Dimensions, which is grounded in the foundation of Habit 1, we engage with others in the system as fully rounded people. Habit 3, Looking for What's Unseen; Habit 4, Working with Cracks; and Habit 5, Experimenting a Way Forward, enable us to discover and realize opportunities for transformation. Habit 6, Collaborating with Unlike Others, focuses on working across differences to advance more powerfully. Practicing Habit 7, Persevering and Resting, is a resilient and joyful way to sustain the journey over the long haul. The conclusion, "Begin Anywhere" suggests ways to start and to continue moving.

Each of the seven habit chapters closes with a simple everyday practice that you can work with, and the book ends with a discussion guide that you can use with others to deepen your understanding and practice.

This book will help you grow your capacity to engage radically and to contribute to transforming systems. You can do this. We can do this.

ACTING RESPONSIBLY

A system produces the results it is producing because the people who are part of it continue to play the roles they are playing. Radical engagement starts with acknowledging where we are: accepting and taking responsibility for the roles we are playing and for those we need to play—not just doing what is expected of us or whatever we like. We become part of the solution by becoming aware of how we are part of the problem, and acting accordingly.

CARING FOR ALL OUR RELATIONS

Marcia Anderson is a medical doctor and the vice-dean for Indigenous health, social justice, and anti-racism in the Faculty of Health Sciences of the University of Manitoba. Her professional biography, before it lists her academic and public health accomplishments, says that she "is Cree-Anishinaabe and grew up in the North End of Winnipeg, with family roots in the Norway House Cree Nation and Peguis First Nation in Manitoba." She is conscious of the people and places she comes from and is part of, and this consciousness provides a basis for her work to transform the health system in Manitoba.

I interviewed Anderson about her work on dismantling systemic racism in health and health education—on transforming rather than just tweaking this system. She explained that racism is manifested in the system's visible policies, procedures, and practices, which are driven by its invisible underlying culture, beliefs, and paradigms—and that changing the latter involves people who are part of the system transforming themselves and their relationships with one another.

When I asked her why she had chosen to do this challenging work, she answered by telling me a startling story about her father having had a heart attack while she was a medical resident.

My dad had a massive heart attack when he was forty-nine. It was terrible: he actually drove himself to the emergency room and had a cardiac arrest at the triage desk. I was at home after a Critical Care Unit rotation, so at that time I was living and breathing heart attacks. My mom called me and just said that he had collapsed, and so I went in to the hospital not knowing anything else. He was in the resuscitation room and was not being appropriately treated. The reason why, even though he was in obvious, clear, severe shock, was that they assumed he was drunk; they said that right to my face, not knowing that he was my father. So I had to intervene, and I took over my dad's care, ordered the sedation, ordered the tests, had someone call the angiographer, all of that. Very clearly he would have died if I wasn't a doctor and hadn't been on that rotation. He did end up making it, after a long and complicated hospitalization.

That moment crystallized my purpose. There's tons

of data about racism in the health care system, but for me, at the end of the day, it's: The next time my dad has a heart attack, is he going to be safer if I'm not with him? Then, in a kind of "all my relations" view, my dad is relatively privileged in having a daughter who's a well-known physician, and that will afford him some safety if he or I can identify our relationship, but that shouldn't be necessary for Indigenous people or Black people or other Brown people to achieve equitable health care.

I was moved by the connection Anderson made between her concern for her father and for others. And I noticed that in telling this story she referred to an "all my relations" view, and I asked her what this meant.

This core teaching, in multiple First Nations languages, is to see everyone as family. It's the difference between seeing the whole community as your relatives versus only your nuclear family. It is one of the reasons why you experience vicarious trauma when you see something happen to someone you identify with: you yourself are traumatized when there's a police shooting involving an Indigenous person, or a report on Indian Residential Schools comes out. There are pluses and hardships that come with this extended view of kin.

So my integrity wouldn't be just to make sure my dad is safer. I'd already done this by virtue of the work and who I am and my recognizability, but I couldn't sleep at night if I didn't extend this more broadly in my extended kinship networks. And a core part of the teaching is this doesn't just refer to human relatives: it refers to the earth, the water, and the other beings as well.

Anderson's understanding of what she needs to do—of her role and responsibility—in the Manitoba health system is informed by her understanding of her relatedness within larger human and more-than-human systems.

SEEING MY ROLE AND RESPONSIBILITY

I first met Anderson in 2018 when we, along with some of her First Nations colleagues and mine at Reos, organized a process in which fifty Indigenous leaders created a vision and pathway for transforming the First Nations health system in Manitoba to produce better and fairer outcomes. (The life expectancy of First Nations people in the province is ten years less than that of other Manitobans.)[1] This process enabled me to see more clearly the terrible results that the Canadian system is producing for Indigenous people, and challenged me to act responsibly given my privileged role in that system.

The first morning of the first workshop of the process immediately revealed a crack in this system, which was represented in microcosm by those of us who were in the room. I was presenting the methodology that our joint facilitation team was proposing, backing it up with examples from my international experience, when George Muswaggon, a former grand chief from Cross Lake First Nation, spoke up in a matter-of-fact voice: "I don't trust you."

I was frightened by this challenge to my presentation—to this cracking of my expertise, which I had assumed was solid. But through this crack I could immediately see why Muswaggon and others in the group didn't trust me and didn't want to go along with the proposal I was making. For centuries in Canada (as elsewhere), Indigenous people have been colonized, massacred, oppressed, marginalized, and cheated by White people, who arrogantly force things to be the way they want them to be. Some of the participants in this workshop thought that I was reproducing this degenerative approach and weren't prepared to accept it. I recognized the roles I was playing in this system— both as an impartial facilitator and as a White expert—and this recognition enabled me to relax and open myself up to changing what I was doing.

A little while later we took a break in the meeting, and while the participants went next door to have coffee, our facilitation team huddled around a table in the meeting room. We were all upset that the participants had rejected our expert proposal. But within fifteen minutes, we had decided to pivot sharply. When the meeting resumed, we took a completely different approach that braided Reos's global methodology with that of the local First Nations: starting and ending every day in a traditional spiritual ceremony led by Muswaggon and others; employing fewer, shorter structured activities to create more space for unstructured dialogue; and having more of the facilitation conducted by the First Nations members of our team and less by Reos, with me coaching from the sidelines rather than directing from the front.

Anderson emphasized the need for us to take this new approach that decentered Reos's methodology by quoting Black civil rights activist Audre Lorde: "The master's tools will never dismantle the master's house."[2] Our team accepted responsibility for the roles we had been playing in the project and the tools we had been using; we changed them, and from then on the project progressed more fluidly and productively, and helped the First Nations health system in Manitoba work better during COVID-19 and afterward. Out of this crack a new way forward grew.

Later I spoke with Muswaggon about our interaction. He told me, "The history of my people means that we cannot dole out trust like candy. But I observed you and prayed and decided that you are a good person. This trust is simple and will last." Our strengthened relationship enabled us to advance the project.

We cannot act responsibly to transform a system unless we understand and acknowledge our roles in that system. My experience in Manitoba of seeing more clearly the roles I was playing nudged me to act more humbly and responsibly in this and other contexts.

During the ceremonial portions of the Manitoba workshops, I heard the elders use an evocative phrase, "All my relations," so I was intrigued when Anderson used it in our later conversation about her work. Then I read the following sentence in an essay by Cherokee writer Thomas King: "'All my relations' is an encouragement for us to accept the responsibilities we have within the universal family by living our lives in a harmonious and moral manner (a common admonishment is to say of someone that they act as if they had no relations)."[3]

King's parenthetical comment hit me. I grew up as a bookish kid in a nuclear family in an individualistic culture. Moving from London to Cape Town in 1993 was therefore a stretch for me: from living on my own without knowing my neighbors to living in a bustling house with my new wife, Dorothy, and her four teenage children in a community where people took a keen interest in their neighbors' lives. Moreover, coming from the United Kingdom to South Africa, working as an expert international consultant, and becoming a White stepfather to Black kids brought into relief my embodiment of the deep hierarchical structures of colonialism, White supremacy, and paternalism. I had to unlearn a lot before I could even begin to adopt a horizontal, all-my-relations view.

I was accustomed to thinking of myself simply as an impartial outsider who helped other people transform their systems. Radical engagement, however, requires us to stretch beyond this comfortable, arm's-length position to grasp the ways in which we are part of these systems—and therefore play a role in them and have a responsibility toward them.

WHAT IT MEANS TO ACT RESPONSIBLY

The first everyday habit for transforming systems generatively is acting with responsibility, not only for ourselves but also for the larger system. What does this mean?

It doesn't mean doing whatever we want or like to do.

It doesn't mean adapting to the system: keeping our head down and staying in line, doing what the system expects of us so that we can thrive within it.

It doesn't mean throwing up our hands, complaining that there is nothing we can do to change things.

It doesn't mean pushing the system to become the way we want it to be, regardless of what others want—that's dictatorial and degenerative.

And it doesn't mean taking responsibility for everything that is going on in the system, like a savior—that's unrealistic and degenerative.

It does mean that, like elephants caring for other members of their herd, we must accept responsibility for our particular relatedness to the system, the role we play in it, and our impact.

What *is* our particular role?

DISCERNING OUR ROLE

We discern the role we can and must play in transforming the system by becoming conscious of where we have come from and with whom we are related—as Anderson's biography emphasized—and, consequently, of where we are now.

Acting responsibly

The foundational everyday habit of radical engagement is to pay attention to the position in the system that we are currently occupying: the role we are currently playing.

What is our position in the system, and to whom are we connected and related? From this position, what can we see and do? Every particular position—geographic and functional, at the center or the periphery, senior or junior—enables a particular contribution to understanding what is happening in the system and to transforming it. For example, when I spoke with Trevor Manuel about the South African transition, our different histories and positions in that system—his as a South African politician, mine as a Canadian facilitator—generated our different understandings and contributions. Just because you're not in control of a system that you are part of (individuals rarely are) doesn't mean that there is no way for you to influence that system; it only means that you have to discern your role and the contribution you can make.

Given our position, what role are we playing in what is happening in the system? Management professor Bill Torbert pointed out to me that the aphorism, "If you're not part of the solution, you're part of the problem" misses an important point, which is that if you're not part of the problem, you *can't* be part of the solution. If we can't see how what we are doing or not doing is contributing to things being the way they are, then our only means of transforming the system is through pushing on it from the outside—and when we do this, our contribution is likely to be either negligible or dictatorial.

The responsible starting point for contributing to systems transformation is to understand the role we are currently playing, the responsibility this role entails, and therefore the role we can and must play going forward. Educator Vanessa Andreotti says, "Our first responsibility is to expand our collective capacity to sit with difficult and painful things, without feeling overwhelmed, immobilized, without placing our hope in quick fixes, and without relations falling apart."[4] Accepting responsibility takes courage and patience.

Businessman Tex Gunning puts such sitting with difficult things at the center of his radical approach to management development.[5] I worked with him when he was the president of Unilever Bestfoods Asia and we were organizing a business–government–civil society alliance to reduce child malnutrition in India. He pushed hard to get his executives out of their privileged, comfortable cocoons to confront the reality of what was going on in their company and society; when I met him, he was sending them to spend two weeks doing frontline community service jobs, such as working as orderlies in hospitals. "It takes wiping shit off people's bums," he told me, "to shake these businesspeople out of their sense of separateness and superiority, so that they take their human responsibilities seriously." Acting responsibly requires humility and openness.

CHOOSING TO ACT RESPONSIBLY

The crucial choices involved in acting responsibly relate to what particular relationships and roles we are acknowledging and accepting responsibility for—both the roles we have been given and those we have taken. In my case, is it my roles as an individual, responsible for myself; as a brother, husband, father, uncle, and grandfather, responsible to my immediate family; as a founder of Reos, responsible to my colleagues and clients; as a writer, responsible to my publisher and readers; as a neighbor, citizen, consumer, investor; as a Montrealer, Canadian, descendent of European immigrants, Jew; as a being entangled with all life? Each of these roles carries with it different opportunities and obligations. "Acting responsibly" is less a recipe than a riddle.

There is no simple correct choice about what relationships and roles we accept responsibility for and to whom we are responsible. As I've said elsewhere, most people don't think they need to transform the systems they are part of (or don't think they're able to), so they accept responsibility only for protecting and advancing themselves and their family or organization, and for living as well as they can within the systems as they currently are.

But many people, including Anderson and others on whose work this book is based, think they can and must contribute to transforming systems, and so accept larger responsibilities. Most of you who are reading this book are also accepting larger responsibilities, and because a system is transformed through the actions of many people in many different positions in the system, with and without formal authority, doing many different things, every one of you, by engaging with those around you and working the cracks within your reach, can contribute to transformation.

Whatever the location and scale of the responsibility we are accepting, doing so means assuming liability and accountability—not making excuses—for our contribution to what is happening. We must take actions based not only on what we need but also on what is needed of us. This takes guts, especially when it implies sacrificing our comfortable or privileged way of seeing ourselves and doing things—which is why we so often deny or abdicate our responsibility. Writer Upton Sinclair said, "It is difficult to get a man to understand something when his salary depends on his not understanding it."[6] Acting responsibly is a moral and ethical undertaking.

THE TWO FACES OF ACTING RESPONSIBLY

To be able to contribute to transforming a system, we must act responsibly—but usually this is not easy or straightforward.

Here is an exercise that I have found to be illuminating: Write two one-page essays about a problematic situation you're dealing with. In the first essay, describe the situation as if you were observing or directing it from the outside; write down in detail what other people are doing that is contributing to the situation being as it is and what those people need to do differently to enable the situation to get unstuck and move forward.

In the second essay, describe this same situation as if you were participating in and cocreating it from the inside; write down in detail what you are doing that is contributing to the situation being as it is and what you need to do differently to enable the situation to get unstuck and move forward.

After you have written these essays, observe the difference in yourself in shifting from the first, outside stance to the second, inside one. People who do this exercise typically observe that in the second essay, when they are taking responsibility for their role in what is happening, they feel more guilty and burdened, and also see that they have more options for what actions they can take and more energy to act.

Taking responsibility for our role creates both more liability and more agency. It nudges us beyond simplistic stories about who is good and bad, right and wrong—beyond heroes and villains.

As most of us know from our family lives, acting as though others are our relations toward whom we have responsibilities produces both joy and suffering—as Anderson described it, "pluses and hardships." In her book *Becoming Kin*, Ojibwe-Anishinaabe writer Patty Krawek observes, "We are all related, but clearly we don't always get along."[7] Acting responsibly involves reducing our separateness and cracking our protective shells, which open us up to both healing and hurt. Acting responsibly, as relations, is life-giving and necessary, but not easy or straightforward.

Acting responsibly involves acting to exert an influence on the larger system beyond the domain over which we have ownership or control. Such stretching can be uncomfortable and even dangerous, and it also enables us to make a bigger difference in the world.

In summary, acting responsibly presents us with both risks and opportunities.

The first and foundational everyday habit of radical engagement, acting responsibly, involves stretching toward answers to—wrestling with—the questions, What are, today, our relationships, roles, and responsibilities in this system? Given these, what can and must we do next? With this habit as with the other six, we need to strive for progress rather than perfection.

AN EVERYDAY PRACTICE FOR ACTING RESPONSIBLY

Here is a simple way that you can practice this first habit every day. You use this practice and those described at the end of each of the next six chapters to work with radical engagement, employing Edward Deming's classic PDSA learning cycle:[8]

- Plan. Choose a system you are part of that you care about and have some influence in, and choose another person who is also part of that system.

- Do. Engage with this person, and on the basis of this engagement, stretch to take one small new action. (The content of this Do step is different for each of the habits.)
- Study. Take note of what happens, inside and around you, as you engage and act.
- Act. Adjust what you are doing to take what you have learned into account.

Although these practices are simple, they are not easy: they require us to act our way into overcoming our inner obstacles to opening, engaging, learning, and growing.

The specific version of the Do step for Habit 1, after choosing a system and person, is as follows:

1. Engage with the other person and, through this engagement, enlarge your understanding of the system, your role and relationships in it, and the impact you are having.

2. Consider what responsibilities your role entails.

3. Stretch to take one small new action that is consonant with what you now understand to be your responsibilities.

Then continue to the Study and Act steps in this cycle, and repeat.

RELATING IN
THREE DIMENSIONS

Transforming a system requires attending to the system as a whole, to its parts, and to the relationships among these parts. Radical engagement entails relating with other people in three corresponding dimensions—as actors playing roles in the system, as parties with our own interests, and as entangled kin—not just in the one or two ways we're most comfortable with. We do this by connecting with others, and ourselves, as fully rounded, three-dimensional beings.

TRANSFORMING THE GLOBAL CLIMATE SYSTEM

One of the most complex and urgent sets of systems transformations humanity must make comprises those demanded by the global ecological and climate emergency. Many people, all around the world, at all scales, playing all kinds of roles—scientists, activists, farmers, city planners, businesspeople, legislators, diplomats—are laboring to effect these transformations. Reos supports some of these efforts, and this is how I met Christiana

Figueres; it was through talking with her that I came to understand how the way we relate with others affects our capacity to effect transformation.

One reason the climate emergency is so difficult to deal with is that it's truly global, with everyone's actions affecting planetary ecosystems and therefore everyone else. The official international forum for hammering out who will do what is the 1992 United Nations Framework Convention on Climate Change (UNFCCC), which includes an annual Conference of the Parties (COP). In 2010, after the fifteenth conference (COP 15) in Copenhagen failed to produce binding commitments to action, Figueres was appointed executive secretary of the UNFCCC, and she directed these conferences for the next six years, culminating in COP 21 in Paris in 2015. She brought together national and subnational governments, corporations and activists, financial institutions and faith communities, think tanks and technology providers, and NGOs and parliamentarians, to jointly deliver the unprecedented, binding Paris Agreement in which 195 countries agreed on a collaborative path to limit future climate change.

Despite this extraordinary diplomatic achievement, however, climate change has continued to worsen. The enormous transformations that are required have started, but so far are not sufficient. In the face of this daunting challenge, Figueres continues to energetically lead civil society efforts to address this crisis.

In my 2021 interview of Figueres, I asked her how she was approaching the climate emergency, and she answered in terms of transforming a complex system.

Food, health, poverty, justice, gender—all of these issues are actually completely interconnected. They are part of the planetary social, economic, and political system that we have built, and nature is our best teacher about this. You can't take one process in nature, one ecosystem, one growth pattern, and say, "This is individually separable from the rest of the ecosystem." What that actually means is that it allows us to be able to approach this complexity of issues through whichever approach is best for the skills we have. If your approach is best for social justice, go at it that way, but know that by going in through social justice, you will be positively affecting soil, oceans, food, health, poverty, et cetera. For me, I chose climate as my approach to this complexity, and I know that climate affects everything else.

Then she explained the particular kind of leadership required to transform such a complex system.

This is not leadership by title or by institution-given authority. That gets you actually nowhere. It is also not leadership to tell everyone what to do, because to begin with, in a complex system you often don't know what to do yourself, so don't even start telling others what to do. Those two options for leadership—let's just take them completely off the table right from the start.

So what's the other option? It's hard to find words for something that was intuitive. I could start with being genuine, being authentic about what we're facing and how we're facing it. This was a very important pathway to connect with myself and to connect with other people, because then I am not talking head to head: then I'm talking heart to heart.

> This is a completely different quality of work that allows us all to put our lack of knowledge, our lack of experience, our lack of solution on the table, and humbly say, "We don't know, but can we figure this out together?" That to me was absolutely the starting point, and then to have what we call in my Buddhist practice a "beginner's mind." Always ask the questions. Always know that you don't know anything.

She seemed concerned that I might be thinking that the whole-systems, openhearted, open-minded approach she had taken meant that she hadn't been paying attention to the details of the negotiating positions taken by different countries and to the cracks these presented, and she quickly added,

> But you also have to know your stuff, right? I mean, we had sixty-seven issues being negotiated at the same time, in five negotiating tracks, with 195 different positions on each of those sixty-seven issues on five tracks, all at the same time. So you have to know exactly what each issue means, exactly what every country position is on each of those issues, exactly how a change in one comma in one track changes a verb in the other track.

Then she emphasized what motivated her sense of responsibility to do this work.

> For the work on climate change, you also have to have a sense of justice, because ultimately, unaddressed climate change is the mother of all injustices. What the Global

North has done is unjust to the Global South. My generation is unjust to future generations. Climate change is unjust to women and children. It is unjust with respect to socioeconomic standing in every country.

The Paris Agreement was the product of epic radical engagement. With the following words, Figueres described the agreement as a beautiful tapestry and identified her responsibility in the process:

> The tapestry has to be woven with many, many different threads, of all different colors, because otherwise it's a very boring tapestry. And so it has to be woven by many people, but if you are in a position of responsibility (which is different than authority), then your responsibility is actually to reflect the beauty of that tapestry to everyone who has contributed to it, because most people are still hanging on to their little thread: "Here's my red thread, here's the blue one, here's the golden one." So your responsibility is actually to say, "Right, you've all contributed to this, and here's what the tapestry looks like, and you can see yourselves represented in that tapestry, but it is not only your red thread or your green thread. It is the threads of everyone." That, to me, is the responsibility of someone who's holding the space for a collaborative effort.

I was surprised by Figueres's characterization of the approach she had taken to leading these long, complex, polarized, high-stakes global negotiations. I had expected her to say that it had been primarily formal, rational, linear, and top-down, but instead she emphasized how it had been informal, relational, synergistic, and bottom-up. I wanted to better understand the ways she had engaged that had enabled her to contribute to the global breakthrough.

HOW SYSTEMS WORK

Figueres's reference to complex interconnected systems prompted me to review what I knew about how systems work and are transformed.

Pioneering systems scholar Donella Meadows writes that a system can be understood as "a set of elements or parts that is coherently organized and inter-connected in a pattern or structure that produces a characteristic set of behaviors, often classified as its 'function' or 'purpose.'"[1]

Meadows gives the example of our digestive system: "The elements of your digestive system include teeth, enzymes, stomach, and intestines. They are interrelated through the physical flow of food, and through an elegant set of regulating chemical signals. The function of this system is to break down food into its basic nutrients and to transfer those nutrients into the bloodstream (another system), while discarding unusable wastes."[2]

In the example of the ecosystem of a savanna, the characteristic behaviors of the system as a whole (for example, cycles of growth and decay) are produced by the many interrelationships among the beings in that system, which include elands, trees under which they shelter, lions that prey on them, vultures that pick at their carcasses, dung beetles that feed on their feces, and so on.

To transform any system, we need to work with all three of these dimensions (now put in the order I will use throughout the rest of this chapter and book):

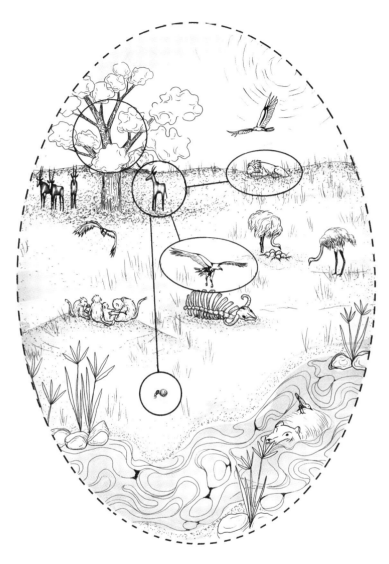

Understanding a generative system

Dashed line: the characteristic behaviors of the system as a whole
Ovals: the elements of the system
Solid lines: the relationships among the elements

1. The system's function, purpose, or characteristic set of behaviors or outcomes

2. Its elements or parts

3. The structure of the interconnections or interrelationships among these parts

We cannot transform a system by working with just one or two of these dimensions. In particular, we cannot transform a system just by changing its elements—for example, by changing other people or ourselves. "A system generally goes on being itself," Meadows says, "changing only slowly if at all, even with complete substitutions of its elements—as long as its interconnections and purposes remain intact."[3] Focusing only on changing individuals is therefore inadequate. Radical engagement focuses on all three dimensions.

Our societal, sectoral, and organizational systems are producing characteristic sets of behaviors that in some cases and respects are wonderful and in others terrible. For example, our fossil fuel–based energy system, which is at the center of efforts to address the global climate crisis, is producing a mixed set of outcomes: abundant, transportable, storable fuel that powers modern societies; enormous wealth for certain people and countries; geopolitical rivalry; supply and price instability; and catastrophic pollution, including climate change. The interconnected structures that produce these outcomes include technologies, infrastructures, organizations, regulations, markets, economic and political interests, geological formations, and ways of thinking. Most of these are well established—some of them literally set in concrete—and not easy to change. And yet many people—solar engineers, renewable-energy entrepreneurs, climate campaigners, government regulators—are working on changing these structures to transform the energy system toward producing different (more distributed and less polluting) characteristic outcomes.

We have created systems and, if we understand how they work, then we can re-create them to produce better behaviors and outcomes. If we don't understand how they work, we can't transform them.

"A system is perfectly designed," medical doctor Paul Batalden says, "to get the results it gets."[4] This is usually not literally true, because most systems are not created or re-created by a single designer all at once, but rather are built up over time as the result of many decisions taken by many people for many reasons. But the aphorism is useful because it encourages us to look at the behaviors or results a system is actually producing rather than only what people say it is supposed to be producing, and to look at the structure of interconnections that is producing these results.

THREE WAYS OF RELATING WITH PEOPLE IN SYSTEMS

My conversation with Figueres inspired me to get more involved in supporting climate work, and in November 2022 I participated in COP 27 (a later edition of the conferences that she had led) in Sharm El-Sheikh in Egypt. There I was able to observe close up the processes of radical engagement that she had described.

This event was one of the largest gatherings in the world to work on one of the most complex and urgent challenges in the world. Thirty-five thousand people, including government representatives, NGO leaders, businesspeople, activists, lobbyists, scientists, and journalists, engaged over two full weeks in innumerable encounters—negotiations, panels, protests, press conferences, workshops, meals, hallway conversations—to find and create openings to accelerate climate action. It was simultaneously a festival of engagement across a handful of bustling venues in a single small beachside city, a formal United Nations negotiation, a research conference, a trade fair, a mass movement, a protest site, a media circus, and a networking extravaganza. I found all of this both uplifting and discouraging: a huge number of committed people were doing their best to address the climate challenge, yet they made only modest progress. I wondered why.

In reflecting on Sharm El-Sheikh, I realized that I had observed the participants relating with one another in three distinct ways that corresponded to the three dimensions in Meadows's definition of a system and that Figueres had referred to in our conversation:

1. Some of them were focusing on *the characteristic behaviors of the system as a whole,* relating with other participants impersonally as *fellow role players or actors* in, as Figueres had described it, "the planetary social, economic, and political system that we have built."

2. Some of them were focusing on *the parts of the system,* relating with others as *fellow parties* who were negotiating in order to reconcile, as Figueres had said, "195 different positions on each of those sixty-seven issues."

3. Some of them were focusing on *the interrelationships among these parts,* relating with others as *fellow beings or kin* who, as Figueres had asserted, have rights and responsibilities vis-à-vis one another in the face of "the mother of all injustices."

Most of the participants in COP 27 were relating with others primarily in one of these dimensions and neglecting the other two. Some were relating in two of the dimensions and neglecting the third. A few, the most effective ones, were relating fluidly in

Relating in three dimensions

all three dimensions—like a group of wolves who are relating in three ways at the same time: (1) hunting as a pack, (2) fighting one another for dominance and food, and (3) cohabiting as family. (In an organizational system, similarly, we can relate with others [1] as team members performing particular functions or jobs, [2] as individuals with our own professional and personal needs, and [3] as human beings.)

The second habit of radical engagement is relating with others as fully rounded, three-dimensional beings: as (1) fellow actors, (2) fellow parties, and (3) fellow kin. Few of the participants in COP 27 were doing this, and this is one of the reasons they didn't achieve much.

DIMENSION 1: RELATING AS FELLOW ACTORS

The first dimension of a system comprises the characteristic set of behaviors of the system as a whole—its actual behaviors, which are often different from its advertised ones. When we are focusing on this dimension—on the good of the system as a whole—we are problem solving, relating with other people in the system as if we were interdependent parts of this whole (not independent parts whose actions don't affect others); we're like actors playing roles in a play or teammates playing positions in a team. This is the typical focus of policy analysts and systems designers.

The first focus of COP 27 was on the behavior of the climate system as a whole. The shorthand for the desired change in behavior was summarized by the conference's unofficial slogan, "Keep 1.5 Alive," meaning acting together to limit the increase in the global average temperature of the Earth's surface to 1.5 degrees Celsius. Many of the policies and actions being proposed were framed in terms of what different actors ought to do to achieve this objective for the good of all, based on the assumption that these actions were in the actors' own interests or could be made to be (through regulatory or financial incentives), or that they ought to take these actions regardless of their own interests (in their "enlightened self-interest"). Countries and companies that were not taking these actions were accused of perfidiously undermining "the good of the whole."

Radical engagement must focus on the good of the system as a whole and on people as actors in that whole. To do otherwise is to ignore the reality of interconnection and interdependence and the danger of fragmentation and polarization. But focusing on the good of the whole is not straightforward—because there is in fact no such thing as "the whole," unless we are referring to the whole.

A "holon" is a whole that is part of other wholes, and one of the reasons that addressing the climate crisis is not straightforward is that different people are focusing on the good of different holons: not only the holons of all life on Earth or all humanity but also those of individual countries and organizations. When a person exhorts others to focus on "the good of the whole," they usually mean the holon that matters to *them*, ignoring those that matter to others.

Focusing on the good of the whole is necessary, then, but never straightforward. It is also not sufficient: if we focus only on the good of the system as a whole but neglect the good of the individual parts and of the relationships among them, then we will suffocate those parts and relationships. For example, an organization that focuses only on the bottom-line health of the organization as a whole but neglects the health of individual employees or departments and of the relationships among them will produce burnout and silos. Transforming systems requires more than focusing on the good of the whole.

DIMENSION 2: RELATING AS FELLOW PARTIES

The second dimension of a system is its parts. When we are focusing on this dimension—on the good of the parts—we are negotiating, relating with others as if we were self-realizing holons, each with our own interests (not assuming that we all have the same interests or that some people's interests can be ignored), like parties in a business or legal or political matter. This is the typical focus of power brokers and deal makers.

The second focus of COP 27 was on such negotiations among parties. The global climate crisis threatens all of us, so we have a general common interest in transforming the climate system, but different people, organizations, and countries have different specific positions, interests, capacities, understandings, and ambitions. Consider, for example, the differences between subsistence farmers in Kenya and coal workers in Germany, between the governments of the US and China, between corporations and activists, and between young students and middle-class retirees.

At COP ("Conference of the *Parties*") these differences among parties were negotiated among the official governmental delegates in their round-the-clock meetings. They were also negotiated in the bazaar-like cacophony of the sprawling unofficial spaces, with thousands of people presenting, proposing, pushing, pitching, and protesting, and through all this activity making agreements and deals so that each could better achieve their personal and institutional interests.

Radical engagement must focus on the good of the parts and on people as parties. To do otherwise is to ignore the obviously important reality of every holon's self-realization, self-protectiveness, and self-interest, and of the real differences among these holons. But focusing on the good of the parts is not straightforward: when every holon is promoting its own interests, this usually—not exceptionally—produces competition and conflict.

Focusing on the good of the parts is necessary, then, but never straightforward. It is also not sufficient: if we focus only on the good of the parts but neglect the good of the whole and of the relationships, then we will produce fragmentation and violence. In an organization, incentivizing only the performance of individual employees will produce competition among them and will compromise the performance of the organization as a whole. Transforming systems requires more than focusing on the good of the parts.

DIMENSION 3: RELATING AS FELLOW KIN

The third dimension of a system is the interrelationships among its parts. When we are focusing on this dimension—on the good of the relationships—we are cohabiting, relating with other people in the system as if we were relatives (not as "others" or objects), like kin with whom we are inextricably entangled. This is the typical focus of peacemakers and community builders, and of the First Nations invocation of "all our relations."

The third focus of COP 27 was on healing and strengthening relationships. Many participants had worked together in and outside of COPs, or were friends or friends of friends, so the event felt like a boisterous community gathering. Lots of participants focused on strengthening connections across different organizations, sectors, issues, factions, and regions, and on increasing the fairness of these relationships in the face of "the mother of all injustices." (Many of the transformations described in this book, including the one in South Africa, have been impelled by this drive to reduce injustice.)

Furthermore, some participants explained their work on climate in terms of their connectedness and kinship with humanity and with the Earth. Indigenous participants Ninawa Huni Kui and Vanessa Andreotti wrote:

> The genuine process of decarbonization is a profound process of reparation of our relationship with the Earth and our relationship with and between ourselves. We need to recognize the repeated mistakes we have made and work with humility towards a new form of coexistence, a new form of relationship with the planet. Without repairing relationships, we will not achieve the necessary coordination for local or global decarbonization.[5]

Radical engagement must focus on the good or health or fairness of the relationships and on people as kin. To do otherwise is to ignore the reality that we are inextricably interrelated, entangled, and living together in a crowded world. But focusing on the good of the relationships is not straightforward: different people often have incommensurately different ideas about who they see as their kin and the right way to live together and to act fairly and justly. And it is difficult to transform social structures when the people who are benefiting from the relational status quo fight to defend their power, positions, and privileges.

Engaging with relationships is necessary, then, but never straightforward. It is also not sufficient: if we focus only on the good of the relationships but neglect the good of the whole and of the parts, then we will produce counterfeit harmony. In an organization, focusing only on the quality of relationships will not produce good individual or organizational performance.

Transforming systems requires more than focusing on the good of the relationships.

RELATING WITH PEOPLE IN THREE DIMENSIONS

The three ways of relating with other people are fundamentally different and equally important. To transform a system effectively, we must know our position in the system and, from this position, take responsible actions (Habit 1) by moving in all three of these dimensions (Habit 2)—just as getting around in physical space requires us to know our starting point and to move side to side, back and forth, and up and down.

When we relate more fully, in all three dimensions, we create more connection, agency, and justice. When we don't, we create more fragmentation, oppression, or inequity.

The three ways of relating are in permanent tension: (1) Which holons are and must be connected? (2) Which holons need to give and get what? (3) How are the holons related, and what way of relating is fair? Systems transformation therefore never moves in an idealized straight or stable line: it always involves constraint, conflict, and compromise.

As I've said, most people favor and focus on only one or two of these three ways of relating, and are therefore limited in their ability to understand and transform systems. To caricature the individuals locked in these one-dimensional efforts: (1) the whole-system designer or policy wonk who treats politics as unfortunate and humanness as unimportant; (2) the power broker or deal maker who treats systems design as impractical and relationships as irrelevant; (3) the community builder or tree hugger who treats systems design as ungrounded and self-interest as misguided.

These one-dimensional efforts are all inadequate ways of working with systems—just as moving only side to side, back and forth, or up and down would be an inadequate way to get around physical space. These three ways correspond to three complementary strategies for transforming systems: (1) "scaling up" by impacting the laws and policies that structure the system, (2) "scaling out" by replicating and disseminating the innovations to impact greater numbers of people, and (3) "scaling deep" by impacting the cultural roots of the system.[6] We will be most effective in engaging radically and transforming systems if we can move fluidly and strategically in all three dimensions.

We practice relating in all three dimensions by paying attention to each of them—not simply by employing our strongest dimension(s) but by stretching and strengthening our most constricted or weakest one(s). Each of us has different strengths and therefore requires a different program of stretching. I was trained in and am good at (1) analyzing the behavior of whole systems and facilitating the collaboration of actors from across a system for the good of that system as a whole. I understand and am comfortable in (2) mediating the differing, even conflicting, interests of different parties—although less so when I am one of those parties. And I have been slower to grasp the central importance of (3) acting responsibly and fairly in relationship with kin (Habit 1), both because I grew up in an individualistic culture and because I have generally experienced systems as working well and fairly for me. So my learning to engage in all three dimensions has been a gradual, intentional process of stretching and strengthening.

Polymath Johann Wolfgang von Goethe said, "Man knows himself only to the extent that he knows the world; he becomes aware of himself only within the world, and aware of the world only within himself. Every object, well contemplated, opens up a new organ within us."[7] As we learn to relate with others as fully rounded, three-dimensional persons we become more fully rounded ourselves, and as we unblock these dimensions in ourselves we unblock our engagement with others. Inner and outer change are like two sides of a Mobius strip, where each one leads to the other.

The second everyday habit of radical engagement, relating in three dimensions, involves stretching to relate with others as fellow actors, fellow parties, and fellow kin.

AN EVERYDAY PRACTICE FOR RELATING IN THREE DIMENSIONS

Here is a way to practice Habit 2: a particular Do step in the general Plan-Do-Study-Act cycle described at the end of chapter 1.

1. Engage with another person who is part of the system.

2. Notice which dimension(s) of your relationship you are emphasizing: relating as a fellow actor, as a fellow party, or as kin.

3. Stretch to take one small new action to emphasize a dimension that you have been neglecting.

LOOKING FOR WHAT'S UNSEEN

A system cannot be fully grasped from any single perspective or position. Radical engagement involves seeing more of what's happening by looking from multiple perspectives—not just from those we're accustomed to and comfortable with. We sense more by stretching to seek out and learn with people located at other positions in the system.

ENGAGING TO DISCOVER A NEW WAY FORWARD

The third and last of the 2021 interviews that motivated me to write this book was with former Colombian president Juan Manuel Santos. I found it both revealing and unsettling.

In 1993, inspired by my experience at Mont Fleur, I moved to South Africa and began to work as a facilitator of systems transformation processes. In 1996 I traveled to Colombia, at that time in the middle of the longest-running internal armed conflict in the Americas, among the military, crime syndicates, right-wing paramilitaries, and two left-wing guerrilla armies. When Santos had been minister of foreign trade, he visited South Africa and met with his hero, Nelson Mandela, who suggested that Colombia might find it useful to undertake a process like that undertaken at Mont Fleur. Santos spoke about this with businessman Manuel José Carvajal, and they and others invited me to facilitate a process called Destino Colombia (Destiny Colombia), which brought together leaders from across the system—politicians, businesspeople, trade unionists, farmers, and combatants from all sides—in nine intense days of dialogue dedicated to looking for ways to end the war.

The workshops, held in a small countryside hotel protected by a ring of soldiers, were the only occasion when leaders of all of these groups, locked in this decades-long violent conflict, peacefully met, talked, listened, argued, ate, drank, joked, and played soccer and music. They created a microcosm of the country they wanted.[1]

Two decades later, Santos, at that point president of Colombia, signed a peace accord with the largest of the guerrilla groups (the FARC, the Spanish acronym for the Revolutionary Armed Forces of Colombia). By this time the conflict had killed 450,000 people and displaced eight million. Santos was awarded the Nobel Peace Prize for "his resolute efforts to bring the country's more than 50-year-long civil war to an end."[2] On the day his award was announced, he characterized Destino Colombia as "one of the most significant events in the country's search for peace."[3]

The peace accord was the culmination of years of fighting and negotiating, and Santos was both celebrated and vilified. I once met him in his office and asked him how he was, and he replied, sardonically: "As well as can be expected as the president of a country like this."

During our 2021 interview, I asked Santos about an experience that I had heard him describe as formative, when as a young man in the Colombian Navy he learned to sail a small boat. He replied,

> I use the analogy of sailing because no matter where you are and how the winds are against you or in your favor, you always need to know where you want to go. So in life, in governing the country, in managing an enterprise, you need to have your destination very clear. And if you do have your destination very clear, then you can use the winds against you in your favor.

I have also sailed small boats and so understood what he meant: one of the most thrilling maneuvers is to position your boat and sails and body so that the wind coming toward you pushes you forward instead of backward. Santos's point was that we can't control the context we are in, but if we are alert and skillful, then in any event we can find opportunities to advance toward our objective.

Santos had fought the FARC ferociously and then signed a peace accord with them. I asked him about the difference between making war and making peace.

> It is much easier to make war than to make peace. I had the possibility of doing both. I made war as minister of defense, and quite effectively: I was elected president with the highest margin in Colombian history because I was a war hero. And to change from a hawk to a dove is a very traumatic change in the political arena, and they started calling me a traitor. Because they had elected me as a war hero, many people said, well, as a war hero, you're going to finish off your adversaries, your enemies. But the best way to finish off your adversaries or your

enemies is to make peace with them. Then they cease to be your adversary or your enemy. That transition is very difficult to understand in the minds of many people, and you need different types of leadership.

Leadership in times of war is quite easy: vertical leadership, you give orders, you rally the forces behind you, and you go against your adversary. In making peace, that type of leadership doesn't work: you need a different type of leadership; you must become a teacher, you must persuade—for example the victims—to accept a peace process. And I thought that that was going to be very difficult. It wasn't that difficult, but it's another type of leadership, with more compassion, with more empathy.

I was intrigued that in Santos's experience it was easier to get things done through war than through peace: that forcing was easier than engaging. Like Manuel and Figueres, he was explaining the particular, engaged way of being, relating, and acting that is required to be able to effect transformation generatively.

I told Santos that one of the things that had most surprised me in the Destino Colombia workshops was that the participants who had been most personally affected by the conflict—one person's sister had been kidnapped, another's son had been killed, a third had been living between safe houses, and so on—seemed the most open and committed to working for peace. He replied,

Something similar happened to me. I thought that the victims would be the most reluctant to accept the peace process, precisely because they were victims, they had suffered, and they would be reluctant to approve a process that would give legal benefits to the perpetrators. A former professor of mine at Harvard came to Colombia

and visited me and said to me, "You're taking a very difficult road, and you will be alone and feel alone. One
reenergizer could be to talk to the victims to ask them
what happened to them and what their feelings are."
And so I started doing that, almost as a matter of discipline, almost one victim a week. And I discovered that
they were the most generous.

After telling me about all kinds of atrocities that had
happened to them and their families, they would say:
"But Mr. President, you must persevere, don't throw in
the towel, you must continue." I asked them, "Why are
you so generous? And they said something which was
very important: "Because we don't want others to suffer
like we suffered." And that really was a lesson of compassion and empathy that was very important for me.

I thought that Santos's choice to engage so diligently with
victims of the conflict revealed an exceptional openness to the
most painful aspects of the reality that he was trying to transform. I was touched by what he was saying, and asked him how
he had been changed personally by these experiences.

Well, I've changed a lot. I have become more sensi-
tive to social injustice, more compassionate, and more
empathetic. I have also become much more aware of
the necessity of making peace with nature. I had had
experiences as minister of defense with our Indigenous
communities. Before that I had sort of ignored them, as
many people do, but I started hearing from them about
their philosophies, their culture, their knowledge, and
I started admiring them, and understanding why they
claim certain rights. And so I decided to make a gesture

to the Indigenous communities, and before going to Congress to be inaugurated, I went to the leaders of the Indigenous communities and asked for their permission to become president. That was a gesture that moved them, and so they become my allies, and they gave me a sort of mandate: You must make peace among Colombians, but you also have to make peace with nature. Because nature is mad, and she's going to retaliate, and you're going to suffer the consequences.

It was striking that as Santos advanced, he kept engaging fresh perspectives on what was going on and what he could do: Mandela, the participants in Destino Colombia, voters, adversaries, his former professor, victims, Indigenous communities. One of the simplest ways for us to see more of what we are not seeing is to engage with people who are positioned at other places in the system and are therefore seeing it from different perspectives. This process is easier to describe than to do. Santos did it.

THE HARD EDGE OF RADICAL ENGAGEMENT

One of the unusual features of the Colombian peace process was that the government and the guerillas negotiated a peace accord while they were still at war—that is, without first having agreed on a ceasefire. Santos said,

We negotiate as if there is no terrorism, but we continue to fight terrorism as if there is no negotiation. That is very difficult, especially when you have to confront public opinion, because people criticize you: How are you in a conversation with these people who are committing these atrocities? Why do you keep sitting down with them? Well, the answer there is that, if you have the military balance of power in your favor, that serves as a good stick, because in a negotiation you have to have a carrot and a stick. And this is a very important stick to press for a solution.

He was explaining a crucial point that many facilitators and peacebuilders overlook: in engaging with others, we usually get things done through a combination of both carrots and sticks. This can be overt, as in the extraordinary case Santos was talking about, or covert, as in most more ordinary cases. Working things out among parties (Dimension 2) requires a hardheaded and sometimes strong-armed focus on interests. Systems transformation is not for the fainthearted.

Then Santos told a story that I had never heard before:

One of the most difficult questions and difficult decisions was when I had agreed with the FARC to certain rules of the game. As I mentioned, we did not have ceasefire: we continued the war and negotiations at the same time. Well, it happened that while we were in that process, a military commander called me and said, "We have the leader of the FARC located. Will you authorize an operation against him?" And you can imagine how difficult that decision was: this was the leader with whom I had been exchanging messages in starting the peace process. But I had told the FARC, and I used these very blunt words: The rules of the game are that you can kill me, and the process shall continue. For the peace process to be successful, I needed the support of the military, and this leader was the highest-value target for the military. So I decided to allow the operation, risking that the rest of the FARC would simply break off the negotiations. But they didn't, because they said: Yes, President Santos told us that we could kill him, and that would be part of the rules of the game, so he is complying with that. It's very difficult, but it's the truth. That was a very difficult moment.

In his roles both as minister of defense and as president, Santos had used violence to advance toward peace. As in his sailing example, he had done what he thought he needed to do to achieve his objective given the particular context (including the rules of the game) and opportunities that he was facing.

I was shocked by this story, and it enabled me to see something crucial that I had not been seeing about the dynamics of transformation. The process of transforming a system that is held in place by established parties and interests involves not only collaboration and compromise but also conflict and coercion. Transformation requires pragmatism rather than purity. Radical engagement is rarely serene, straightforward, or safe.

SEEING WHAT'S UNSEEN IN THREE DIMENSIONS

One of the basic requirements for transforming systems is to be able to see what is happening and how things work, not only from our own familiar and comfortable perspective but also from the perspectives of other people in other positions in the system—including perspectives that are unfamiliar or uncomfortable for us. Writer James Baldwin said, "Not everything that is faced can be changed, but nothing can be changed until it is faced."[4] If we aren't willing and able to face the system, then we won't be able to transform it.

Habit 1 involves understanding our own position; Habit 2 involves acting from that position through relating with others in three dimensions (as actors, parties, and kin); Habit 3 involves facing more by seeing more, through the eyes of those others.

In 2012, Santos said about Destino Colombia: "It is truly breathtaking to read the scenarios now because they seem more prophetic than academic."[5] The thirty-four members of this team were able to see the future so perspicaciously because they looked at the Colombian social-political-economic-cultural system from an unprecedented diversity of positions in that system. (Throughout this book I use such hyphenated multidimensional descriptions of societal systems, which are never one-dimensional.) Although they continued to have profound disagreements, they all came to see and understand more. And many of them recall the intense and open encounters with others whom they had most hated and feared as among the most significant experiences of their lives.

The Destino Colombia team faced their reality directly, and this enabled them to act more effectively. During one workshop session, businessman César De Hart said that he had firsthand experience of the conflict with the guerrillas, did not trust them at all, and believed that the country's best hope for peace would be to intensify the military campaign against them. It took courage for him to say this because he was directly challenging not only the guerrillas but also the rest of the team and their hopeful belief that a peaceful solution was possible. He was willing to be frank, and by then the team had worked together for long enough and their relationships were strong enough that they were able to hear such a statement without rupturing. Furthermore, when De Hart said exactly what he was thinking and feeling his words cleared the fog of conceptual and emotional confusion that had filled the room, and we could all see clearly this mistrust and the possibility of intensified conflict that it implied.

Seeing more enabled the team to engage with the behavior of the system as a whole (Dimension 1): to together grasp more of what was happening and could happen. This interaction led to the team's elaborating a scenario—a story about how different actors might act—that was called "Forward March!" In this story, the government, supported by a population frustrated with the continuing violence and operating from the principle that "a hard problem requires a hard solution," implements a policy of crushing the guerrillas militarily.

Seeing more also enabled the team to engage with the interests of the parts—of the different parties (Dimension 2). When I spoke with Colombian intellectual and politician Antanas Mockus about the project, he said that some businesspeople and landowners, having concluded that "Forward March!" was the best option for themselves and for the country, had promoted it as a blueprint to the government of Alvaro Uribe (in which Santos had been minister of defense), and this government had in fact, to widespread acclaim, implemented just such an aggressive crackdown. "We must not fix our attention," Mockus said, "only on the conviviality of such dialogue processes. We must not forget the harsher external world where scenarios can be chosen to guide action." The team's conversations enabled different parties to adjust and advance their own strategies (including in opposition to the strategies of others).

Seeing more also enabled them to transform their relationships. Jaime Caicedo was the secretary general of the far-left Colombian Communist Party, and Iván Roberto Duque (also known as Ernesto Baez) was a commander of the far-right paramilitary United Self-Defense Forces of Colombia (AUC). During one of the workshops, Caicedo and Duque had stayed up late talking and drinking and playing the guitar with Juan Salcedo, a retired army general. The next morning, Caicedo wasn't in the meeting room when we were due to start, and I asked the group where he was. They made jokes about what might have happened to him. One person said, "The general made him sing." Then Duque said, menacingly, "I saw him last." I was frightened that Caicedo had been murdered, and was relieved when a few minutes later he walked into the room—he had overslept.

Later I heard a revealing coda to this story. A few years after this workshop, Duque had gone into the jungle to meet his boss, Carlos Castaño, the notorious head of AUC. Castaño excitedly told Duque that AUC fighters had discovered the location of their archenemy Caicedo and were on their way to assassinate him. Duque pleaded for Caicedo's life, telling Castaño the story of that evening together at the scenario workshop and saying, "You can't kill him; we were on the Destino Colombia team together!" They argued and then Castaño called off the assassination. I see this story as exemplifying the transformative potential of engaging as kin (Dimension 3). Duque had transformed his relationship with Caicedo and his understanding of what acting responsibly entailed in this situation: fighting to save his enemy's life.

SEEING NEW POSSIBILITIES

One of the contributions of Destino Colombia was that, during a pessimistic period when Colombians could not see any way to transform the reality of their apparently permanent conflict, the team envisaged not one but multiple possible scenarios. One scenario was of the conflict continuing: "When the Sun Rises We'll See," a warning of the chaos that would result if Colombians failed to address their tough challenges. But the team also imagined three possible ways it could be transformed: "Forward March!", which I mentioned earlier; "A Bird in the Hand Is Worth Two in the Bush," a scenario of negotiated compromise between the government and the guerrillas; and "In Unity Lies Strength," describing a bottom-up transformation of the country's mentality toward greater mutual respect and cooperation. Santos described his presidency as enacting "In Unity Lies Strength."

William Ury, the negotiating expert who advised Santos throughout the peace negotiations, writes in his book *Possible: How We Survive (and Thrive) in an Age of Conflict*, "Conflict is natural. In fact, we need more conflict, not less—if we are to grow, change, evolve, and solve our problems creatively. While we may not be able to end conflict, we can transform it—unleashing new, unexpected possibilities."[6] Ury says that one element of Santos's approach was to "swarm" the conflict with many different perspectives and contributions, including those of the Destino Colombia team.

The peace accords did not end the conflict in Colombia, but they did transform it, in some respects, toward nonviolence. The Destino Colombia team, Santos, and others envisaged and enacted a more peaceful future that had previously been invisible. They contributed to making possible a future that had been seen as impossible.

SEEING FROM THE PERSPECTIVE OF
PEOPLE WHOM THE SYSTEM IS HARMING

In our 2021 interview, Santos placed a striking emphasis on the role in building a new, more peaceful system that could be played by the victims of the old violent one—the millions of people whose families had suffered death, injury, or displacement at the hands of various armed actors. Santos had been inspired and informed by his weekly interactions with these people, but I wasn't clear about why this mattered so much.

Through my work in Colombia, I had met Francisco de Roux, a Jesuit priest and peacemaker who in 2017 was appointed chair of Colombia's Commission for the Clarification of Truth, Coexistence, and Non-Repetition (a body mandated by the 2016 peace accords). After the Commission had completed its report, attacked from both left and right, de Roux went to Boston College to recover and reflect, and in 2023 I drove down from Montreal to spend a morning with him.

I asked him about his experiences in the Commission, and he immediately answered: "I was in contact with victims, from all sides, for 1,400 days." Because he said 1,400 days, not five years, I inferred that he was emphasizing a daily habit, like the daily Ignatian spiritual exercises that Jesuits practice. I wanted to know why he was emphasizing this, so, taking the risk that he would think it a stupid question, asked him why this mattered.

De Roux paused as though he was trying to find a way of answering that I could understand. "It was important for me to engage with victims," he said, "in order to connect to reality. They understand better than anyone the dynamics of the political violence that was at the center of the Commission's work." I grasped de Roux's analytical point: that to understand more fully the reality of a system and how to transform it, we must center the often-unheard voices of actors whom the system, intentionally or not, is excluding, marginalizing, obscuring, and oppressing—those whom the system is failing or against. This means decentering the usually dominant voices of the elites for whom the system is working.

Then de Roux went on.

I also do this to connect to my own vulnerability. We all feel frightened and vulnerable because we know that we can get hurt and will eventually die, so we put up walls to protect ourselves. In order to create a country that works for everyone, we must remove these walls. The victims can be immensely powerful through enabling other people to access their own vulnerability. People don't want to see the truth of what is happening, but the ethical power of the victims can awaken their own ethical behavior.

(When, during this conversation, de Roux and I spoke about personal matters, I was impressed that even at eighty years old he was still stretching and growing. And when I asked him for advice on a matter that was troubling me, he demurred, saying only, "That's a choice you'll have to make." Acting responsibly requires each of us to keep feeling our way forward.)

As we lower our walls—crack open our shells—we become better able to engage with others and to act responsibly, not simply as actors or parties but also as kin. And engaging with others enables us to lower our walls even further—with all of the possibilities for pain and joy that this entails.

REMOVING THE OBSTACLES TO ENGAGING RADICALLY

This was not the first time de Roux had pointed me to a profound aspect of the work of systems transformation. In 2017, one week after he had been appointed to the Commission, my colleagues and I facilitated a workshop with diverse leaders from across the war-torn southwest region of Colombia.[7] I was surprised to see de Roux at this out-of-the-way event just as he was starting his important new job, but he explained that he thought he might be able to learn something useful from the process.

During the first day of the workshop, the leaders made good progress in coming together across their deep divides and, as we broke for dinner, de Roux came up to me, excited: "I see what you are doing! You are removing the obstacles to the expression of the mystery!" The mystery he was referring to was not the kind in a mystery movie that gets solved at the end but something that is intrinsically unknowable. This enigmatic hint inspired me to write, in *Facilitating Breakthrough*, that the role of the facilitator is not to *get* people to collaborate but rather to remove the obstacles that are impeding them from doing so.

In order to develop the habits required for us to engage radically, we don't need to weld something new or foreign onto ourselves. We need "only" to remove the obstacles or shells that we have erected to protect ourselves, thereby becoming more open and vulnerable and thus more capable of expressing the capacities for engagement that we already have within us. When we remove these obstacles, we can see and face more—including those things that we have been most frightened to face. Such work to overcome our inner obstacles is a challenging and lifelong endeavor.

LEARNING TO SEE WHAT WE AREN'T SEEING

As I have described in this chapter, the essence of the habit of looking for what we are not seeing is stretching to see not only from our own position but also from the positions of diverse others. We can never understand everything about anything (if for no other reason than because everything is always changing), but we can stretch to understand more. This habit is important for transforming any kind of system, whether a country, community, organization, or family.

My university physics and economics studies and my first jobs in research institutes and companies trained me to calculate and advocate confidently, even arrogantly, for the single correct answer to any difficult question. But in 1988, when I was twenty-seven years old, I joined the strategic planning department at Shell and began a different kind of training: to see from multiple perspectives. Our team's job was to challenge the strategic thinking of the company's executives to enable them to see more and therefore make better decisions. We did this by constructing multiple scenarios about what could happen in the future based on multiple interpretations of what was happening in the present.[8] This job introduced me to practices focused on looking for what's unseen.

The core challenge of seeing what we are not seeing is to escape from our habitual blinkered interpretations: seeing what we are used to seeing, or are directed to see, or are rewarded for seeing. Pierre Wack, the founder of the department, "had studied some of the mystic traditions of India and Japan in depth, had been a student of the Sufi mystic G. I. Gurdjieff in the 1940s, and he had learned to cultivate what he called 'remarkable people' around the world; this phrase in French means not so much gifted or eccentric people, but people with unconventional insights about the world around them."[9] Wack understood that an effective way to see what you are not seeing is to have it pointed out to you by someone you respect who has a different position in and perspective on the system.

This discipline of seeing with clear eyes was drilled into me by all of my Shell bosses. On my first day in my new job, department head Arie de Geus came into my office and with a flourish showed me the empty shelves and cabinets, saying that he had removed all of my predecessor's files because he wanted me to contribute a fresh perspective.

One of our primary methods for gaining fresh perspectives was to talk with diverse others—a basic way of engaging. I told my immediate supervisor, Ged Davis, that I had met with a person whose views didn't make any sense to me, and he advised me that I could always learn something new if I remembered to remain curious and attentive to what the world looked like through the eyes of the person I was talking with. And I once conducted a long interview alongside my boss, Kees van der Heijden, and was astounded afterward: when we compared our notes, I saw how much more he had heard than I had because he had been so much more disciplined in writing down everything that seemed important to the interviewee—not filtering out, as I had, statements that didn't seem important to *me*.

Later I assisted Joseph Jaworski, van der Heijden's successor, in conducting an interview during which he spent over an hour asking the interviewee about his personal history. I found this boring, and afterward asked Jaworski how he had succeeded in feigning interest; he replied, amazed at my fundamental incomprehension, that the key to engaging with people was to be truly interested in them. We increase our understanding of what is happening and what we must do, and our capacity to do it, through deepening our relationships. (Yet there are many things that all of us, including or especially those of us in elite positions like the one I had at Shell, do not understand and even do not *want* to understand.)

I once organized a training for my Shell team that was conducted by violinist Miha Pogacnik. He played a short piece of classical music and then asked us what we had heard. One of my colleagues answered, "I liked it." Pogacnik responded: "I don't care whether you liked it or didn't like it! Tell me what you heard!" He wanted to teach us to truly listen to and appreciate variations in the music's tempo, color, mood, and energy. Our biggest impediment to listening and understanding is to rush to judge whether something or someone is good or bad, right or wrong, hero or villain. Judging short-circuits sensing.

Through all of this rigorous training, I developed the third habit of radical engagement: engaging with diverse others with genuine humility, curiosity, discipline, openness, empathy, and respect—and thus seeing more of what is happening.

These are the orientations that, on my good days, I have brought to my work as a facilitator. In the Mont Fleur workshops, I modeled such engagement, and this supported the participants to see together, across their deep divides, more of the South African system they wanted to transform. The inventive insight of the organizers of Mont Fleur had been to compose that team of people from across the system. This approach was unlike the one we had taken at Shell, which was to assemble experts from a single location in the system (the company) plus other experts to advise us. As a collective, the Mont Fleur team could see from many angles, which was similar to looking from multiple angles to see a stick insect hidden in a tree (while also inquiring into why the insect is hiding and why we are overlooking it). Team member Howard Gabriels said about their conversations,

> The first frightening thing was to look into the future without blinkers on. At the time there was a euphoria about the future of the country, yet a lot of those scenario stories were like "Tomorrow morning you will open the newspaper and read that Nelson Mandela was assassinated" and what happens after that. Thinking about the future in that way was extremely frightening. All of a sudden you are no longer in your comfort zone. You are looking into the future and you begin to argue the capitalist case and the free market case and

Looking for what's unseen

the social democracy case. Suddenly the capitalist starts arguing the communist case. And all those given paradigms begin to fall away.[10]

This habit of looking to see what we are not seeing is, like all the habits, easier to write about than to do. I have found, over and over, that I am not seeing (and sometimes don't want to see) something happening in a system I am part of, and I usually become aware of this only through having it brought to my attention—sometimes angrily and pointedly, sometimes quietly and in passing—by someone whose different position in and experience of the system enable them to see something that I am not. More than once, my wife, Dorothy, has told me that someone is discriminating against her, and I have thought that she was imagining it. We all have things that we are not seeing, and we must stretch beyond our comfort zone to be able to face and grasp more of what is going on. Denying what is going on is acting irresponsibly.

The practice that I have found most useful for developing this habit is to be alert, open, and curious about what, compared to my current thinking, is different or surprising—as I was in reflecting on the three interviews that inspired this book. Scientist Charles Darwin paid particular attention to such disconfirming data: "I had, also, during many years, followed a golden rule, namely, that whenever a published fact, a new observation, or thought came across me, which was opposed to my general results, to make a memorandum of it without fail and at once."[11] We see more when we have the curiosity, openness, and discipline to take note of signs of our having failed to see.

The third everyday habit of radical engagement, looking for what's unseen, involves stretching to seek out and engage with people who have positions in and perspectives on the system that are different from ours. This can be both challenging and thrilling.

AN EVERYDAY PRACTICE FOR LOOKING FOR WHAT'S UNSEEN

Here is a way to practice Habit 3: a particular Do step in the general Plan-Do-Study-Act cycle described at the end of chapter 1.

1. Engage with someone who is in a position in that system that is very different from yours.

2. Observe, without judging, how their perspective on what is going on in the system is different from yours.

3. With this enlarged perspective, stretch to take one small new action.

HABIT 4

WORKING
WITH CRACKS

Systems are structured to keep producing the behaviors and results they are producing, and therefore often seem solid and unchangeable—but they are not. They are built, and they collapse. They crack and are cracked, which opens up new possibilities that some people find frightening and others find hopeful. Radical engagement involves looking for, moving toward, and working with these cracks—not ignoring or shying away from them. We do this by seeking out and working with openings, alongside others who are doing the same.

SEARCHING FOR OPENINGS

Al Etmanski has pioneered the transformation of the living conditions of Canadians with disabilities, away from segregation, dependency, and second-class status toward connection, agency, and justice. I have spoken with him and studied what he and others have written about his decades of experience, and especially about how his strategy and approach have evolved and enabled him to make the contributions he has. He has advanced through repeatedly searching out and working with openings or cracks (breakdowns and bright spots) in the social-economic-political-institutional-cultural "disability system."

Etmanski has spent most of his adult life as a community organizer, at the beginning as an educator, youth worker, and social housing planner. When his second daughter was born with Down syndrome, he became a parent activist in the disability movement.

> I soon became head of the largest disability rights group in British Columbia (BC), and our activism produced a string of successes, including the closure of BC's three large institutions for people with developmental disabilities, all its segregated schools, and many of its segregated classrooms and sheltered workshops. We blocked roads, sued government, and won an important right-to-treatment court case. This all gave birth to what is now called the community living movement.
>
> For me these advances were tarnished by two realizations, one personal and the other cultural. First, my warrior mentality had taken its toll. I had become the very dragon I'd set out to slay. I left behind me a trail of busted relationships, particularly with government but also with some of my colleagues. Second, although the physical institutions were closing, an institutional mentality still occupied society's collective psyche. People with disabilities were no longer segregated, but they were not part of their communities. Pity, charity, and low expectations dominated. Society neither recognized people with disabilities nor expected them to become contributing members of society.[1]

Frances Westley is a leading scholar of systems transformation who has written about the evolution of Etmanski's work.

Al Etmanski has spent his career working to try to find opportunities for disabled individuals. He started out, as many people do, with trying to create opportunities for his own child. He was an organizer in his early days, so he did the classic thing of getting a group of people together in his basement and thinking about what can we do to ensure that our children are safe and secure. They start to do that and they came up with this idea to create a kind of circle of support for people who were disabled, so it wasn't just the parents that they were counting on. His model is very successful and, like in many voluntary or social sector organizations, at a certain point he and his partner Vickie Cammac were running faster and faster just to keep up with the demand. They were exhausted. There weren't really more resources for them, and they were just having to do more themselves.

And so he finally realized that he could do this his whole life, but the system wasn't going to change. In fact, if he wasn't doing the heavy lifting, chances are the whole thing would collapse. So at that point, he made the choice to move to the system level.

He parsed it out, and one area was cultural: he began to bring in people who are cultural influencers, whom he engaged in dialogues with disabled people. And he tracked the extent to which this notion of belonging starts to appear in their work, and was quite successful in influencing them to get the message out for him.

But that wasn't enough in itself, because he also needed to find a way to change the economic situation of disabled people. Canada has had generous support by some lights, but what it did was it treated disabled people as if they were welfare recipients. A welfare recipient earns just under the poverty line. And the law had it that you couldn't get any additional money from other people without the government clawing it back. That really condemned the disabled person to a life of poverty.

Al said he would like to create something called a disability savings plan, to be created as an instrument where anyone who's associated with the disabled person, or the disabled person themselves, can put money into a fund for this individual, and that individual can draw it back. And he said, on top of that I want the Canadian government to buy into this, to match this, so that every $1000 that we put in the government puts in $3000.

In order to do this, Al had to start dealing with a whole different group of people, including with people in the federal government. He had a method, which was whenever a new federal cabinet is appointed, he goes and finds out if anyone has a disabled family member, it doesn't matter what cabinet position they're in, but he contacts them and starts to work with them. And so then when he wants to get something into policy, he has an internal champion in the federal government that he can go to.

And they were successful. This disability savings plan went into effect, which meant that people who had a disability could now draw on funds without a reduction in their disability payments. He got all the big banks in Canada to sign on to this and the government agreed to match it. And it was very subversive because it started to undercut welfare law. Welfare law hasn't changed yet, but there's a growing momentum around the basic income movement in Canada, which I think is likely to be successful. And a lot of that was triggered by the softening and subversive effect of getting this particular legislation in for disabled people, because it questioned the rules.

Now, you know, you're talking about him working over a twenty-five-year period to go from that first stage onward. This didn't happen overnight.[2]

Etmanski has engaged radically, and by doing this succeeded in fundamentally changing the characteristic behaviors of the system. He has related with others (1) as actors whose actions are creating and re-creating the structure of the system as a whole (its institutions, laws, and culture); (2) as parties, including his sometime opponents in government, each of whom have their own political, economic, and social interests; and (3) as kin, attentive to the importance of family and community belonging and the need to strengthen it—not only for disabled people but for everyone. He has contributed to transforming the system by searching for and working with cracks at the system's neglected periphery.

Etmanski told me that the essence of his approach to engaging is to open his heart.

Some people would call this a mindset, but I call it a heartset. You can talk about the importance of relationships or relationship-based fundraising or advocacy or public policy, but if you're not careful that can be very utilitarian, so to have an open heart in these contexts is really important. By this I mean authentic relationships with people: not coming in there to peddle, but being genuinely interested and breeding trust.

The truth about vulnerability or dependency is that's who we are. And so I try to rally the lovesick and the brokenhearted. The broken heart can open you up and provide an opportunity for other people to plug that hole in their heart.

Etmanski's explanation of how opening up to authentic connection enables systems transformation echoed what Francisco de Roux and Joseph Jaworski had told me. Acting responsibly requires breaking ourselves open, or being broken, and thereby becoming able to engage with others, not only as actors and parties but also as kin. It requires being openhearted—but not fainthearted.

HOW SOCIAL INNOVATION WORKS

Westley and her colleagues at the Waterloo Institute for Social Innovation and Resilience have done groundbreaking research on systems transformations in Canada, the US, and elsewhere.[3] Their widely used definition of social innovation—"a new program, policy, procedure, product, process, and/or design that seeks to address a social problem and to ultimately shift resource and authority flows, social routines, and cultural values of the social system that created the problem in the first place"—emphasizes that the purpose of such innovation is to transform the structure of a system so that it produces new characteristic behaviors.

Westley emphasizes that systems get transformed by many actors at all scales, attentive to opportunity, "managing and facilitating the emergence of creative solutions and the marshalling of those solutions to create disturbance and ultimately transformation."[4] I find this general, inclusive, emergent theory of change more plausible than those that posit a singular linear formula: do this and the system will be transformed. Westley says,

> When a social innovation has a broad or durable impact, it will be disruptive, i.e. it will challenge the social system and social institutions which govern our conduct, by affecting the fundamental distribution of power and resources, the basic beliefs that define the system, or the laws and routines which govern it. While there are many smaller innovations continually introduced at all scales, our focus is on those with the potential to disrupt and change the broader system.

Social innovation requires a variety of actors, working in concert or separately, if it is to have the kind of impact suggested above. Among these are the inventors, sometimes called social entrepreneurs, individuals who initiate or create innovative programs, products or processes and seek to build an initial organization that can bring that innovation to market. However, equally key to social innovations that have the broad impact we describe above are the institutional entrepreneurs, those individuals or network of individuals who actively seek to change the broader social system through changing the political, economic, legal or cultural institutions, in order that the social innovation can flourish.

But in complex systems, no change can be accounted for by agency alone. Agency must coincide with opportunity that is a feature of the broader social and institutional context. Social innovation can be aided by market demand, which is one form of such opportunity. It can equally be aided by political demand, another form of opportunity, or by cultural demand in the form of a breakdown in sense making or meaning.[5]

Systems get transformed through the actions of both social entrepreneurs and institutional entrepreneurs who are able to seize opportunities—to work with emerging cracks—as these arise. Westley uses the same image as Santos to characterize the leadership required in such contexts.

We tend to prefer the image of the leader on the charging stallion, to that of the sailor trying to navigate stormy seas. The leader on the stallion seems to be in control of his destiny, while the sailor has no chance of controlling a stormy sea. The sea is too powerful to overcome with force and too unpredictable to reliably anticipate. Instead, the sailor needs to be adept at reading the weather, understanding the patterns, reacting to changes and adjusting his sails.[6]

Working with cracks requires reading the weather: attending alertly to what is shifting, even unexpectedly or subtly; waiting for openings, even small or brief; and then moving decisively and with agility to advance.

CRACKS PROVIDE OPPORTUNITIES FOR TRANSFORMATION

The alternative to trying to transform a system quickly by charging at it, forcing it, or sledgehammering it is to work patiently with and on its cracks as these arise. Cracks present opportunities—leverage points at which we can usefully engage. A rock climber ascends by using cracks or seams in the rock face for finger- and toeholds. The Japanese art of *kintsugi* repairs broken pottery with gold, highlighting rather than concealing the cracks.

A crack is an indication that the system is not as solid and seamless as it might seem—that, in at least in some respects or for some people, it is not working (it has weaknesses) and that, if it were transformed, it could work better (it has possibilities). Nonprofit leader Mary Pickering told me,

> Change-makers need to understand and monitor and utilize cracks. Examples of cracks include informal systems, like barter, that run alongside and try to correct problems in the established system; situations where the inequity of the established system is put into stark relief, like COVID; and technological disruptions, like smartphones, where the way we exchange information is transformed for better and for worse.

A crack is an opportunity for fundamental change, which some people will find hopeful and others frightening; people who want to maintain the status quo don't like cracks and try to ignore or paper over them. In South Africa in the late 1980s, new economic pressures and the end of the Cold War created cracks in the apparently solid apartheid system and hence offered opportunities and risks, toward which Mandela, Trevor Manuel, then-president F. W. de Klerk, and others had the imagination and courage to move. They hospiced the old system and midwifed a new one, and by 1994 the country had, in fundamental ways, been transformed.

In 2020, COVID-19 cracked Reos Partners' established service model, which was based on facilitators and participants traveling to in-person workshops. Within a month we transformed our model to virtual and hybrid delivery, which turned out to be both more economical and more accessible.

Clara Arenas is an activist and researcher in Guatemala with whom I have worked during that country's hopeful ups and horrifying downs. She told me that she and her colleague Marco Chivalán realized that "even among the cracks and ruins (including those created by capitalism and colonialization), small plants can grow, and as they grow can widen the cracks and bloom into new ways of being in the world." Transformation grows in and from cracks.

A crack can show up as a problem and/or as an emerging solution; as a wound and/or a site of healing. A crack often appears at the edge of a system or on an underlying fault line. It can start small and faint and be ignored, and can grow suddenly and quickly and then no longer be ignored. It can lead to the whole system collapsing and/or transforming.

Acting responsibly to transform a system (Habit 1) and engaging it in multiple dimensions (Habit 2) and from multiple positions (Habit 3) enable us to better notice and work with its cracks (Habit 4).

Westley describes the impetus for the founding of Etmanski's organization, the Planned Lifetime Advocacy Network (PLAN), as a response to a crack: the disability system was not working for many people with disabilities and their families. "Like so many innovations," Westley writes, "PLAN began with a sense that something had to be done. The system had failed them, but out of this failure the families took heart, not despair. There had to be a better way."[7]

She says that the work of system transformers unfolds through their seeing and choosing to move through such cracks (or, as Westley puts it, doors): "Social innovators are not people

Working with cracks

who create more doors, or even people who are surrounded by more doors than other folks. They are simply people who see more doors. They believe in doors, if you will, and so doors are there."[8] When we engage radically, we are alert to cracks as opportunities for transformation.

The increasingly broad and deep system transformations that Etmanski has contributed to over the decades have grown out of a succession of cracks that he has noticed and worked with. He understands all of these to be symptoms of a broader and deeper crack in Canadian society: a weakening of belonging, solidarity, and caring. Such cracks are often ignored because the dominant system sees the status quo as solid and unchangeable and the cracks as illusory or irrelevant.

Working with cracks is the everyday activity of everyone attempting to transform systems peacefully. Wouter Jurgens is a Dutch diplomat who has spent years attending to difficult and dangerous conflicts across Europe, the Middle East, Africa, and Asia. He and I were discussing different peacebuilding efforts we were involved in, and I noticed that almost all of his stories were of informal conversations to discover new options: with governmental and nongovernmental actors, allies and opponents, through back channels, in one-on-one encounters, at unofficial workshops, during breaks in meetings ostensibly about other subjects. Jurgens is constantly searching for previously unseen shifts and openings—for cracks.

OUR CRACKING SYSTEMS

Our world is always changing, these days more quickly and fundamentally as we breach more ecological and social limits; clearly, many of our systems are cracking. But these systems, which we're used to thinking of as solid and stuck, aren't: they're fluid, and we can transform them if we can work with the cracks and openings produced—sometimes purposefully and sometimes accidentally, often unexpectedly—by this fluidity. Philosopher Bayo Akomolafe writes,

> It seems like things want to fall apart. It seems like we've been stolen from home. Where do you go when things fall apart, when home has been taken away from you, when the cracks appear? . . . The flows and possibilities that proceed from the moment when things no longer fit [are matters] of irruptions and eruptions, breakthroughs, cracks, flashes, fissures, fault lines, discontinuities, blasts, splits, rifts, ruptures, seismic shifts, world-ending openings, miracles, strange encounters, and the yawning maw of a monster.[9]

Change produces cracks and opportunities for transformation.

The Canadian universal health care system is cracking and collapsing. It used to work well for most people, and now it doesn't work well for anyone; even at elite dinner parties, people fret about not being able to find family doctors. David Price is a family physician and medical school professor who works with individual patients, health professionals, and government policymakers to find ways to address this crisis, and who wrote an important expert advisory panel report on primary care. He told me,

> I have no idea how to transform the health system at the macro level: it's pretty complex. I used to think, naively, that writing a thoroughly evidence-based research report with broad recommendations might be enough. The only

way I have found that actually works is through developing long-term relationships with multiple people, including patients, clinicians, frontline workers, bureaucrats, politicians, and medical association and nursing union leaders, to understand what is driving them and what they need. In this way I have had some success, albeit slow, in nudging individuals and the system to evolve.

Working with a system's cracks means feeling for, discovering, and nudging them; making them visible and prying them open; and flowing, growing, or breaking through them. We can't do this if we engage with the system inattentively, at arm's length or superficially, rigidly, and always in the same way from the same direction, seeing and doing the same thing over and over. We can only do this if we engage it alertly, hands-on and under its surface, approaching it fluidly in multiple ways from multiple directions, learning about it and ourselves.

MOVING TOWARD CRACKS

A crack in a system is a sign that, at least for some people, it is not working. A crack offers a not-yet-realized opportunity to transform the system so that it works better for more people; it presents hope, but also disruption, confusion, conflict, and danger, so moving toward it requires courage.

Often we are afraid of cracks, so we ignore, deny, or avoid them. But engaging radically means doing the opposite. As civil rights activist and politician John Lewis said, "When you see something that is not right, not fair, not just, say something! Do something! Get in trouble, good trouble, necessary trouble."[10] Former McConnell Foundation president Stephen Huddart expressed this same impulse when he described to me one of his everyday practices for enabling systems transformation:

> I look at a problem or crisis as an opportunity to engage that I need to move toward, pay attention to, unpack, and relax into. Being relaxed enables us to be present with a problem and to learn about its behaviors and propensities without prompting early, reactive alarm and defensive maneuvers among those who depend on things being the way they are. This enables a systems innovator to find potential allies inside the problem, who will welcome and align with efforts to transform it. The learning, empathy, and trust that this relaxing into the problem enables are what inform subsequent strategy. This has worked so often for me that it has become second nature.

My colleagues and I supported James Newcomb of Rocky Mountain Institute (RMI) in organizing the Electricity Innovation Lab to accelerate the deployment of renewable and distributed sources of electricity. This initiative brings together players from across the system, both "incumbents" and "insurgents"—electric utilities, start-ups, technologists, regulators, and environmental, community, and consumer groups—to come up with and try out new solutions. The Lab has contributed to the upending of electricity markets, and the system has transformed quickly, with the share of renewables in US generation having doubled over the last decade and continuing to increase. I asked Newcomb what he and his colleagues did on a daily basis that made a difference, and he replied: "We kept watching the news for interesting examples of shifts, such as unusual situations or innovative companies, that were illustrative edge cases that were setting new patterns, and we spoke and wrote about these. In this way we made the case for and inspired the transformation we thought was necessary and possible." Through constructing and spreading a new narrative, the RMI team widened the cracks and accelerated the transformation.

The fourth everyday habit of radical engagement, working with cracks, involves stretching to attentively move toward and through cracks, including by engaging with imaginative and courageous others—troublemakers, entrepreneurs, innovators, artists, visionaries, young people—who are doing the same.

AN EVERYDAY PRACTICE FOR WORKING WITH CRACKS

Here is a way to practice Habit 2: a particular Do step in the general Plan-Do-Study-Act cycle described at the end of chapter 1.

1. Engage with someone who is also paying attention to what is changing and cracking in the system.

2. Building on this engagement, move toward a crack and observe it closely.

3. Stretch to take one small new action to explore, enlarge, or move into or through this crack.

EXPERIMENTING A WAY FORWARD

Transforming a complex system requires learning through doing—not just thinking and then doing. Radical engagement involves experimenting: trying things out that we're not sure will work, paying careful attention to the results, and adjusting accordingly—not just doing what is familiar or safe. We discover what is possible through working with our hands and feeling our way forward.

LEARNING WHAT WORKS THROUGH TRIAL AND ERROR

Sumit Champrasit is the founder of a nonprofit organization, Mr. Hope Comes Home, which is reinvigorating rural areas in Thailand by helping young people who moved away to the cities create good livelihoods back home. I met Champrasit in 2010 during a period of violent conflict between pro- and antigovernment movements; he thought that a dialogue that brought together leaders of different parts of Thai society (similar to the dialogues I had facilitated in South Africa and Colombia) could prevent this conflict from worsening, so we started to work together.

I spent many days with Champrasit, driving through dense Bangkok traffic in the back seat of his minivan, he on the phone nonstop. We went to meetings in offices and homes and restaurants to organize this dialogue, with leaders of the two opposing movements, cabinet ministers, members of parliament, generals, company CEOs, NGO leaders, academics, and aristocrats. Champrasit has been a businessman, civil servant, and head of a royal sustainability institute, and is well connected across Thai society. On other days, we would work in the project office with his team of fellow volunteers, each contributing what they were good at and all committed to creating a better Thailand, with lots of joking around and great food. Champrasit knows how to engage.

I worked with Champrasit and his team for ten years on different Thai dialogue processes related both to general political-institutional challenges and to specific ones related to education, agriculture, and corruption. Our whole body of work probably cushioned the national conflict and helped prevent a civil war. And many of the things we tried didn't work, so we kept adjusting and kept trying different things.

In the course of doing all this work, Champrasit discovered a crack, a problem and possibility on which he could act to transform a key aspect of Thai society: the rural development-economic-agricultural-environmental-cultural system. When I asked him how he and his team had developed this Mr. Hope project, he emphasized how they had found their way forward through practical problem solving and hands-on experimentation.

I spent almost two years traveling around the country to see what was really happening. I talked with a lot of people, and found out that the average age of farmers is fifty-eight years old (much higher than the average of the Thai population) because the young people leave home and never return. To reform the agricultural sector, you have to get to the bottom of the systems thinking iceberg, below the events and pattern and structures, to the mental models. We can't reform it with the government spending tons of money every year to guarantee prices or help when there are floods or a lack of water. No one is really solving the root cause of the problem: that there is no new generation who can adapt to a new way of working. The government spends a lot on training, but given the average age of the farmers, it is difficult for them to change. So it is a mental model issue: the attitude that farmers are poor, poorly educated, really weak, and in heavy debt—not reforming, only waiting for subsidies. That's where the Mr. Hope idea came from.

We trained participants in our project through a five-day workshop and then five months of follow-up. One of the major problems with trainings is that the young people go back without any experience and try to implement what they learned. But in reality they have different approaches, different issues, different fundamentals, and so you cannot copy one solution for all cases. That's why the five months is very critical, with five to eight people in a group and a coach that keeps an eye on them, helping them and them helping each other with day-to-day problem solving.

In agriculture you have to test the solution to see if it will be suitable for your own situation, because everywhere, every time, every issue is specific. So there is nothing that is right or wrong until you prove that it works.

We face different problems all the time: different issues with different causes. So we also use system thinking to see how to solve it whether at the event or pattern or structure or mental model level.

Next year will be the tenth year of the program and our approach has been: we adapt, we adapt, we adapt. By the fourth year we started to see the attitude of the young generation toward agriculture clearly changed to be more positive. At the beginning almost all of our graduates were pushed back to the cities by their parents, who said, "Why are you coming back? We spent a lot of money to support your education: now you're making a good salary and you are sending money home to us. Why are you coming back to try something that can't succeed?" By the fourth year we could see changes, with people choosing agriculture as their university major moving from last on the list of majors to the middle. The level of appreciation of the profession of the farmer has totally changed.

We see the end together: our goal. We believe that natural agriculture will become the mainstream once we get to a critical mass of 20 percent of agricultural families, which would be one million families. But we cannot train one million Mr. Hopes ourselves, so we are training change agents. A good change agent can turn around one hundred people in five years, so our goal is to train ten thousand good change agents. So we are clear on the number and we are clear on the method and we are clear on the move-on spirit.

When you understand the way to do things and you see the result, that it really works, you realize that even if what you're doing is only a small move, you have to just keep going, keep on doing it, and one day you will be there. We understand that we're doing the right thing every day, even if it's a small success, and when we have problems we find solutions. We never give up.

I asked Champrasit for a specific example of his key principle that "there is nothing that is right or wrong until you prove that it works," and he answered:

In our first year of running five-day training workshops, we included a half-day "learning journey" to a Folk Philosopher Center that was close to the workshop venue. It was good for our participants to hear the impressive success stories of the folk philosophers, but they wanted to copy those models without realizing the importance of the particular ecosystems of their own home towns. And the duration of these visits was too short for each folk philosopher to share the failures and painful experiences they had had on the way to their successes. Furthermore, the folk philosophers did not really understand what we were trying to do in our workshops: to transform the mental models of the participants so that they could be successful when they returned home. So we changed our selection of workshop venues to choose ones that could be not only training centers but also incubation homes, and who would comply with our workshop process and not try to lead participants to copy any particular success model.

Champrasit moves forward entrepreneurially in his non-profit activities the same way he does in his business activities: taking actions, risking his time, money, and reputation; paying

Experimenting a way forward

attention to what happens; and adjusting accordingly, again and again. He knows that progress matters more than perfection. Over the years, I have seen him pivot many times, as some of his efforts have succeeded and others failed, sources of funds have been won and lost, governments have been enthusiastic and lost interest, and allies have come and gone. At one point he had a health crisis; he told me, "It forced me to experiment with changing how I was eating, drinking, exercising, and sleeping." In all of these realms, Champrasit advances through disciplined trial and error, like an octopus trying out different ways to hide and to catch its prey.

EXPERIMENTING TO DISCOVER WHAT'S POSSIBLE

Jerry Granelli was a great "free jazz" drummer and meditation teacher who knew a lot about outer and inner manifestations of creativity. We were once talking about systems change, and he surprised me by exclaiming: "There's too much loose talk about changing things! I spend most of my time dealing with things that I cannot change!"

Not everything is possible—and also, sometimes, things that seem impossible turn out not to be. The serenity prayer attributed to theologian Reinhold Niebuhr provides wise guidance: "Lord grant me the serenity to accept the things I cannot change, the courage to change the things I can, and the wisdom to know the difference."

Radical engagement involves exploring, experimenting, discovering, and shifting the boundary between the possible and the impossible. This is the opposite of assuming that things can only be the way they are now and that we must keep doing what we have always done.

Experimenting means that we don't know what will work and that sometimes what we try won't work. Furthermore, taking actions to disrupt or replace the status quo is always risky because in most systems, power and resources are aligned with the status quo, and conformity and caution are rewarded. Taking disruptive actions that might not work is therefore doubly risky.

And yet: experimenting is the only way to transform complex social-political-economic-cultural systems like those discussed in this book. Jane Davidson is a politician who was responsible for the government of Wales making sustainable development its central organizing principle. She told me,

> It's all about failing. When the National Assembly for Wales was created in 1999, we had a constitutional duty to promote sustainable development. We were very proud of this duty and wanted to exercise it well. But we failed, because it's not just about adopting a scheme or new ways of working: a fundamental rethink has to happen.
>
> We tried all sorts of mechanisms. When I took on the role of minister of environment, I got Cabinet to agree to make it our central organizing principle of government. And yet things were not changing: a lot more words were used, but really it was the ultimate in greenwashing.
>
> I realized we had to have a duty not just to promote but to deliver sustainable development, and we'd have to learn on the job what that looked like. So I took an emergency resolution on long-term thinking to the Labour Party manifesto conference before the 2011 election and got it through, and that generated the process that became the Wellbeing of Future Generations Act, which was the first of its kind in the world.

In terms of failing forward, all the work that we had done in these ten years to try and understand what we wanted to be able to do became immensely useful because the next administration, who had to make this legislation deliver for future generations, was able to learn from these years of trying to make this work to navigate which pathways had promise and which didn't.

Facilitator Chris Corrigan, citing management consultant David Snowden, defines a situation as complex (rather than clear, complicated, or chaotic) when cause and effect can only be understood in retrospect, so the actions that will be effective in changing the situation cannot be known in advance.[1] Corrigan writes,

> For complex problems, get a sense of possibilities and then try something and watch what happens. You can get advice from others, talk about it with friends and strangers, read blog posts and tweets, but the bottom line is that you need to get to work and learn as you go, engaging in a rapid iterative cycle, and see if helpful patterns emerge. As you learn things, document practices and principles that help guide you in making decisions. Don't worry about collecting tons of information before acting: it won't help you past a certain point. Act on a hunch first and monitor the results as you go.[2]

Complexity requires trial and error and lots of experiments. Snowden uses the phrase "Probe-Sense-Respond" to capture this idea. Basically, because you can't know what will work, you try a bunch of things and see what works. If you are getting better results, you do more of that. If things aren't working well, stop doing that.

In complexity, conflicts get resolved by people DOING things, not arguing over them. We can make better decisions when we have some data that comes from action. If people have different ideas about what to do, invite them to take on small experiments to see if their ideas are promising. You can even have people do two opposite things—"we'll take the high road and you take the low road"—and see how they compare. Experimenting with action is a far better way to find promising practices than constant arguing about the "right" thing to do.[3]

Corrigan emphasizes that when we are exploring and experimenting in a complex context, not everything is possible: "An elephant will not produce a codfish as its offspring, nor will a thistle grow from an apple seed."[4] A system has constraints that both limit and enable what we can do: a wall, for example, can prevent us from advancing in a certain direction and can also protect us from being disturbed; some constraints can be moved and others can't. A system also has affordances that provide opportunities for action: a chair affords the opportunity to sit down.

Just as a tailor must know the particularities of the cloth they are working with, we can only make effective contributions to transforming a system if we know its particularities—especially its constraints and affordances. Champrasit emphasized this when he said, "In agriculture you have to test the solution to see if it will be suitable for your own situation, because everywhere, every time, every issue is specific."

We get to know a system through choosing to work with it responsibly (Habit 1), doing so in three dimensions (Habit 2), seeing it from multiple perspectives (Habit 3), moving toward the places where it's cracking (Habit 4), and probing what's possible (Habit 5).

Radical engagement involves feeling our way forward to discover, open up, and work with cracks. Chinese leader Deng Xiaoping used a memorable image to describe taking such an approach to China's transition toward a socialist market economy: "We are crossing the river by feeling for stones."[5]

I have engaged with social entrepreneur Negusu Aklilu for five years as he has worked to build peace in Ethiopia through periods of promising progress and terrible regress. I asked him what he had learned from this experience and he answered, "Peacebuilding is like cleaning a sheep's stomach to make tripe for food. This is a painstaking process of small steady successes, along with some pleasant and unpleasant surprises. Unlike with other parts of the sheep's body, there is no quick method: it requires patience and perseverance."

These two metaphors of feeling for stones and cleaning a stomach, like those of carving, weaving, and sailing used by Manuel, Figueres, and Santos, are evocative images of engaging radically with a system: taking part in it alertly, hopeful, curious, horizontally, leaning forward, hands-on, digging deep, persisting, and above all reciprocally and relationally. Radical engagement enables us to advance, in touch with the system, one step at a time.

IMAGINING THAT THE SYSTEM COULD BE OTHERWISE

During 2023, Champrasit and I worked with a group of former government officials and military officers from the US and China on how to prevent a continued deterioration in the relationship—even a war—between their two countries. Over the course of an intense four-day workshop (which included moments of extraordinary openness and heartfelt connection) and then four months of emails, the group constructed a set of four scenarios for the relationship: stories about what could happen (narratives they judged to be realistic and plausible)—not predictions about what will happen and not proposals about what should happen. The question about what was possible was therefore front and center in their deliberations.

All four of the scenarios that the group agreed were plausible were characterized by increasing separation and conflict between the US and China. In making this collective judgment, they explicitly decided that a scenario of increasing connection and collaboration was not plausible or realistic: that the domestic and international constraints and affordances in the US-China system made this too risky for the parties and therefore could not happen.

Many of the participants, especially those from the security establishments, didn't trust the members of the other side and feared appearing, to them and also to their own side, to be too soft, flexible, or weak. They argued that the reality of the system precluded improvements in the binational relationship—as if admitting the possibility of improvement would cause them to appear naïve and unrealistic.

If we are loyal to one "realistic" or "official" story about how things are and have to be—in this case, a story of danger and defensiveness—then we will not be willing or able to see other possibilities: we will deny the existence of cracks that might reveal other futures. Such a conservative vision of what is possible or even discussable is not the province only of government officials and military officers; I worked recently with progressive US democracy activists who were also unwilling to engage with unorthodox framings, perspectives, actors, or scenarios. This is why Frances Westley argues that the key step in social innovation is "getting to maybe," and William Ury that transforming conflict requires creating "the path to possible."[6] Creating something new requires being willing and able to imagine that things could become other than as we currently see them.

I was frustrated with the meager results from my work on these US-China relations and US democracy projects. Both of these complex challenges of course demand systems transformations that can't be accomplished with any single project. So I, like the project participants, need to keep regrounding myself in the particularities of each situation, including its constraints and affordances and my role and responsibility in it, and reimagining how things could become other than as I currently see them. The habit of experimenting a way forward is, like the other six, a habit for breaking habits: for engaging afresh with where we are and what we can do next. As of this writing, I haven't yet found any promising next steps to take on these two challenges. Sometimes we can't see what we can usefully do, and so need to wait alertly and patiently for a workable crack.

CREATING NEW REALITIES

Artist Jeff Barnum taught me how to create a path to possible. I noticed that when the two of us were both facing a situation that was disorganized, full of not-yet-reorganized potential, I would feel uneasy and he would feel energized. I once watched with amazement over fifteen minutes as he and some friends transformed a collection of driftwood and stones on a Northern California beach into a gigantic, beautiful sculpture: they had an extraordinary capacity to imagine and enact what could be.

Barnum showed me a film made from time-lapse photographs of Pablo Picasso creating a painting of a matador.[7] Picasso starts out by making a few rough marks on the canvas and then adds detail and color. He changes and paints over what he has done, again and again. At one point he paints over a beautifully rendered bull's head that is right in the center of the piece.

Barnum points out that at the outset of a creative process, we cannot yet see what we will create; it's around the corner. We have an idea of where we are trying to get to (for example, a system that has been transformed), but we don't know how to get there. The word *creativity* is used so loosely that we often forget its essential meaning: to bring forth something that does not yet exist, like the sculpture on the beach.

The discipline required to discover a way forward is to try something out, step back and look at the result, and then change it, iterating over and over. I learned this discipline through writing: even if I spend months thinking about and outlining what I want to say, it is only when I write it down and look at what I have written that I can know what makes sense and what I need to rewrite. I wrote this book through engaging with five hundred or so members of a "Book (Creating) Club" that I had set up, who via Zoom calls and Google Docs provided input and feedback on many iterations of the text. And during the course of this process, I deleted a beautifully rendered "bull's head" from the text: a conceptualization of Habit 2 that I had painstakingly developed over a year but that was no longer working. Creating requires being willing to destroy.

I can create a good text only by recreating a bad one a hundred times. To get going, I must push myself to write a bad first draft: to take a first step.

Creating something new requires being able to look at a still-inadequate and still-incomplete result without becoming frightened ("I am a failure!") or attached ("This *must* be right!"). We need to be present with what is actually happening rather than what we wish would happen. We need to be able to maintain our equanimity in a conflictual, uncomfortable situation where we don't know how things will turn out, or when, or whether we will succeed. Poet John Keats called this "negative capability," which he defined as "being capable of being in uncertainties, mysteries, and doubts without any irritable reaching after fact and reason."[8]

One of the reasons experimenting a way forward in systems transformation is both thrilling and daunting is that it requires us to undertake this kind of patient and relaxed experimentation and iteration—and to do so not only privately, like a painter or poet, but together with others, on issues that really matter to us, risking having our mistakes exposed publicly. To transform a system, we need to have the courage to try something out, learn, and try again.

In transforming systems, the way forward will rarely be clear or straightforward. It is not a highway: we can't clear away the obstacles and make a straight road before we start. We can advance only through rapid, disciplined, agile, iterative experimentation. The systems crises we face create pressure for decisive and definitive action, but advances will not always be linear or predictable. As I suggest in the simple exercises at the end of each habit chapter, we need to undertake many cycles of small steps to learn what works and to build our confidence, capacity, and momentum.

Transformations are usually messy and unclear, especially when we are in the middle of them. We need to be prepared for confusion, crisis, failure, frustration, setbacks, and disappointment (as I experienced during the Thailand, US-China, and US democracy projects). When these occur, we need to pause, sense, and try something new. We need to be open to changing course or to stopping and then perhaps starting off again in a completely different direction.

Experimenting a way forward requires stretching to do things that might not work. Most of the important lessons I have learned in my work and life have not been through succeeding but through failing. Sometimes we are fortunate to be in "safe to fail" contexts. Other times we are, unfortunately, in punitive or precarious contexts where failing is dangerous.

The fifth everyday habit, experimenting a way forward, involves stretching to try things that might fail. We try to fail early when the stakes are low, and to fail forward by learning and improving with every attempt. This is how we can advance.

AN EVERYDAY PRACTICE FOR EXPERIMENTING A WAY FORWARD

Here is a way to practice Habit 5: a particular Do step in the general Plan-Do-Study-Act cycle described at the end of chapter 1.

1. Engage with another person in the system who also wants to transform it.

2. Through this engagement, develop a hypothesis about a possible way forward.

3. Stretch to take one new small action to test this possibility.

COLLABORATING WITH UNLIKE OTHERS

Transforming a system requires actions by multiple people with multiple capacities in multiple positions—not just by one person or organization. Radical engagement involves collaborating with unlike and unlikely others, making our differences productive—not just with people we like, and not forcing or feigning amiability or agreement. We do this by stepping up our engagement from just talking to also acting together.

TRANSFORMING SYSTEMS THROUGH WORKING WITH DIVERSE ALLIES

Rosanne Haggerty is an internationally recognized leader in developing innovative strategies to end homelessness. She is president of the nonprofit Community Solutions, whose Built for Zero movement, which is active in more than one hundred cities and counties in the US, focuses on achieving functional zero, meaning that homelessness, when it occurs, is rare and brief. Fourteen communities have achieved this goal for at least one target population, and forty-four have achieved measurable reductions in homelessness. They have achieved this through collaborating with unlike others.

Community Solutions and Built for Zero approach homelessness as a systems transformation challenge.

> In many American cities, homelessness is widespread. You see it everywhere and for some, it seems almost inescapable. But did you ever wonder why? It's not just bad luck or individual circumstances. Millions of people go through hard times, lose their job, struggle with a health condition or housing instability, without ever losing their homes. So why do some people manage to keep a roof over their head or get back on their feet right away, while others live unhoused sometimes for years? And why are Black and Indigenous people disproportionately impacted by homelessness and 4 to 5 times more likely to experience it than people who are White? That's because it's not about people's choices or worth: systems make the difference.
>
> The people who experience homelessness have fallen through gaping holes in the social safety net. They're failed by systems that were never designed to serve them. On top of that, systems also dictate what you have to go through to get support. If you lose your home, whether you encounter open doors and get access to permanent housing, mental health support, and legal aid, or whether you run into dead ends in a maze of agencies that don't talk to each other and don't remember you, shelters that only get you through the next day, and wait lists that never end.

But here's the thing: we know that systems got us here and we know they can also get us out.[1]

Haggerty's experience of systems transformation has taught her that she must both repair cracks in current systems and work with cracks to build new systems. She told me,

> Homelessness is a wicked problem. Communities have gotten stuck reacting to one crisis after another and never building an effective operating system to prevent and rapidly resolve housing crises. Failing to match their response to the dynamic nature of the problem guarantees that communities stay in a doom loop of expending lots of effort and getting limited results. But it is not credible for leaders to say, "We're building a system to get out of this mess once and for all" without having a plan to deal with the crisis in front of them.
>
> The challenge is to do both of these activities, because you really can't get the political will and long-term commitment to do the systems change work if you leave the current crisis untouched.

She thinks that doing both of these things at the same time requires changing the story, and that changing the story enables and is enabled by enrolling new and sometimes unlikely allies.

> As communities demonstrate the effectiveness of a systems-level approach, our goal is to reframe homelessness in the public imagination as a community challenge with a proven path forward. Through this lens, it becomes clear that many actors, beyond those who have

usually been involved, have key roles to play. We're asking our local partners, "Who in this community, if they were on side and championing the systems change work, would make everything different, so that you wouldn't be pushing that boulder uphill but would be racing to follow it downhill?"

Often it's the real estate developers, the owners of the sports teams, the influencers who've never been consulted or given a role. It's not that it's going to be easy to get these key people on board, but it's also not like people have tried and failed: it's just never been part of the strategy.

Haggerty does her work through engaging radically in all three dimensions: (1) changing policies, for example on land use, that present systemic barriers; (2) negotiating with a variety of parties, each requiring a particular approach; and (3) tapping into a sense of community and civic pride. She keeps searching for new perspectives and openings, and trying out new approaches. And none of this can be done by her nonprofit alone; she needs to collaborate with new and diverse others.

THE CHALLENGE OF COLLABORATING
WITH UNLIKE OTHERS

We cannot transform a system generatively by ourselves. Engaging radically doesn't only involve taking responsibility for our roles in the system (Habit 1), relating with others in the system as fully rounded persons (Habit 2), looking at what's happening from multiple perspectives (Habit 3), working with cracks (Habit 4), and experimenting our way forward (Habit 5). It also involves collaborating with others—and usually not only with friends and colleagues but also with strangers and opponents (Habit 6). All of the systems transformers whose stories I have told so far—Manuel, Anderson, Figueres, Santos, Etmanski, Champrasit, Haggerty, and others—found that, in order to achieve their transformational objectives, they needed to work with others, including with people they didn't agree with or like or trust, and they succeeded in doing this.

Collaborating with unlike others, be it in teams, partnerships, alliances, coalitions, or networks, is necessary and possible. The opposite is to work only with people who are like us and whom we like.

Collaboration has two faces. Its first face corresponds to the word's first dictionary definition, which is "to work jointly with."[2] The primary reason we collaborate, whether within or among organizations and sectors, is that doing so enables us to accomplish more than we can separately—like the sandpiper bird that is said to eat leeches out of the mouth of the Nile crocodile, to the benefit of both animals (and to the detriment of the leeches: transformation means that some things grow and others die). When we collaborate, we pool our diverse assets: experiences, capacities, authority, money, technologies, ideas, followers. Each of us faces different realities and therefore has different positions, perspectives, and powers. These differences enable us to see more of what is happening in and around the system and to work with cracks and advance from multiple angles.

But the second face of collaboration corresponds to its second definition, which is "to cooperate traitorously with the enemy." We often find it difficult, even impossible, to work with "those others" because we fear that doing so will require us to compromise on matters that matter to us—to risk getting annihilated or swallowed, like the bird by the crocodile.

The central challenge of collaborating, then, is working with,

Collaborating with unlike others

through, and around our differences. But we definitely don't need to and can't collaborate with everyone on everything, so we must choose with whom we will collaborate on what. Such choices about whom we both need and are willing to work with can be excruciating, and can look different over time. Christiana Figueres, for example, used to think she needed to work with oil companies to find solutions to the climate crisis, but more recently thinks that she mustn't.[3]

The core of my and Reos's work over the past three decades has been supporting people in working together with those diverse others with whom they need to and are willing to collaborate. This was the crack that I discovered at Mont Fleur when I witnessed South Africans able to work together creatively and productively across their apartheid-amplified differences, separation, and conflict.

Here is the essence of what I have learned about such collaborating. In all groups of people, there are differences. These differences—even apparently small ones, often especially small ones—produce not only delight and innovation but also discomfort and pain. We can't erase these differences and don't have to: it is often possible and necessary to advance together in spite of, even because of, our differences. If we insist on complete agreement and alignment, we will not be able to advance. I once asked Santos why he mentioned Destino Colombia so often in his speeches, and he replied, "I often refer to this project because it is where I learned that, contrary to all of my upbringing, it is possible to work with people you do not agree with and will never agree with."

We can advance through acknowledging our differences (not forcing or feigning sameness) and embracing conflict as well as connection; acting responsibly; and, with this transformational habit as with the others, experimenting a way forward.[4]

We only need to agree on what we can and must; thus we can keep moving and, through moving, learning. Meanwhile, we need to work together deliberately and patiently to build our relationships, understanding, and trust.

EMPLOYING POWER TO TRANSFORM SYSTEMS

Almost everyone who talks about transforming systems talks about collaborating with unlike others. But one of the reasons such collaboration is harder to implement than to talk about is that it requires working skillfully with power, which many people find difficult, distasteful, or even dangerous. (In my interview with Santos, it was his story about having used his lethal power that unsettled me.) Psychologist James Hillman points out that this difficulty especially afflicts people in "idealistic professions":

> Why are the conflicts about power so ruthless—less so in business and politics, where they are an everyday matter, than in the idealistic professions of clergy, medicine, the arts, teaching and nursing? In business and politics, it seems, there is less idealism and more sense of shadow. Power is not repressed but lived with as a daily companion; moreover, it is not declared to be the enemy of love. So long as the notion of power is itself corrupted by a romantic opposition with love, power will indeed corrupt. The corruption begins not in power, but in the ignorance about it.[5]

Civil rights leader Martin Luther King Jr. was clear about the need to employ power to transform systems and about the "collision" involved in doing so.

Power properly understood is nothing but the ability to achieve purpose. It is the strength required to bring about social, political, and economic change. . . . And one of the great problems of history is that the concepts of love and power have usually been contrasted as opposites—polar opposites—so that love is identified with the resignation of power, and power with the denial of love. . . . Now we've got to get this thing right. What is needed is a realization that power without love is reckless and abusive, and love without power is sentimental and anemic. . . . It is precisely this collision of immoral power with powerless morality which constitutes the major crisis of our time.[6]

A system is maintained as it is through the use and abuse of power, and can be transformed only if the power of the people who want it to be transformed is greater than the power of those who want it to stay as it is. All of us who want to contribute to systems transformation, whatever our position, must therefore find ways to build and employ power. We do this primarily through collaborating with others. Radical engagement works with power and love to collaborate to bring about fundamental change.[7]

COLLABORATING WITH THE POWERS THAT BE

In 2022, I attended the annual meeting of the World Economic Forum (WEF) in Davos, Switzerland. Davos is an emblematic example of the collision that King referred to. It is the most important annual global gathering of the people leading and benefiting from current systems—thousands of top corporate, government, and nonprofit leaders (arriving in the greatest number of private jets of any meeting in the world), plus a few hundred young leaders and social entrepreneurs—at which they talk about cracks in these systems and the tweaks and transformations that are required.

I went to Davos because I wanted to engage with this dynamic. The meeting exhibits all the basic tensions involved in collaborating to transform systems: elites vs. others, included vs. excluded, sameness vs. difference, the interests of the whole vs. those of the parts. I spent time with a group of social entrepreneurs who were there to ally with one another and with powerful establishment participants. They all face the tension Haggerty identified: How do you collaborate with leaders of the current system while building—rather than covering up the need for—a new and better system? They advance through this tricky territory not by standing apart from it, trying to remain unsullied by power, but by practicing their pitches, pushing into the fray of the meeting, and seizing opportunities.

Part of WEF's theory of systems transformation is that alliances among companies, nonprofits, and governments can set standards that create profitable opportunities for transformative insurgents to displace conservative incumbents. (This is how the Electricity Innovation Lab contributed to the rapid transformation of the US electricity system.) The potency of this "stakeholder capitalism" model is that it focuses on the good of the whole (participants as actors) while working with, rather than wishing away, the self-interest of the parts (participants as parties).[8]

COLLABORATING THROUGH CONNECTING

People come to Davos to engage: to network, attend fancy dinners and parties, and make deals and alliances of all kinds. Such connecting with like and unlike others is a crucial ingredient in reconciling power and love to transform systems. But in such busy transactional meetings, participants don't have much space to focus on the good and health of relationships (participants as kin). This third dimension is, however, often the radical key to unlocking the first two, and to the extent that conferences like Davos overlook the third dimension, their potential to contribute to transformation is reduced. I saw the value of the WEF model, but the meeting, like COP 27, reminded me of the importance of relating in all three dimensions.

I learned a major lesson in the power of building relationships and connections in 1994, one year after I had resigned from Shell and moved to South Africa, when I cofacilitated a strategy workshop there with renowned community organizer Ishmael Mkhabela. The workshop was at the University of the North, an apartheid-era institution with a history of conflict between radical Black students and a conservative White faculty and administration.

A few hours into the event, a shouting match broke out between the students and staff. One year earlier, a student had been killed, and now the student leaders in the workshop were demanding a moment of silence in memory of their "martyr." The faculty did not want to celebrate a "troublemaker." The temperature in the room was rising, and my attempts to get everyone to cool down and be reasonable weren't working. I started to panic, and then Mkhabela calmly stepped forward. "I suggest a moment of silence, both for this student and for all the others, students and staff, who have been hurt in this conflict . . . and for those who will come after us, for whom we are doing this work. Let us close our eyes." The room fell silent and the fight dissolved. Mkhabela's words connected the participants to common human ground that underlay their opposing positions.

That evening all the participants got together for a boisterous barbecue that spilled out of the hotel lobby and onto the lawn. I was circulating through the group, drink in hand, talking with the university leadership to get a sense of what was going on and what we needed to do in the workshop the next day. I noticed with irritation that Mkhabela was spending the whole time sitting at a small table in the corner of the lobby talking with one student. As we were walking back to our room at the end of the evening, I asked him what he'd been doing and why he hadn't been focusing on the workshop we had been hired to lead. He replied,

> Obviously, Adam, coming from the corporate world, you don't know much about grassroots organizing. This student, like a lot of young activists, has the terrible habit of speaking from his political party's "we" and spouting their party line. This conversation was a real one-on-one: I talked with him heart to heart about what matters to him and what matters to me. Now tomorrow, rather than there being just me, he will have joined me and there will be two of us. This is how we have always done our organizing work in South Africa and how we have succeeded in changing things here: one person at a time.

Mkhabela understood better than I did that engagement is radical when it enables us to connect deeply, at the level of our purposes. This student went on to play important leadership roles in university and city administrations and national politics; and the University of the North, more than its sister institutions in South Africa, enjoyed years of peaceful and productive collaboration. Changing relationships enabled changing systems.

I spoke about the central importance of relationships with another colleague who works in a different context and culture. Junko Edahiro, a leading Japanese environmental teacher and consultant, told me about work she did in the city of Kashiwazaki to help citizens collaborate to create a better future. Kashiwazaki is the site of seven nuclear power plants—the largest such conglomeration in the world—and ever since these were built, sixty years ago, the residents have been divided between pro- and antinuclear factions. Edahiro told me,

> The people who belong to different camps do not talk to each other. It's not just an opinion, it's an identity, so it's very difficult for people to change their positions and to talk. The mayor engaged me in a three-year project to facilitate a conversation between the two camps.
>
> When we started the first meeting of the committee picked by the city—three people for nukes, three against, two neutral—it was like a funeral: dead silence. Nobody talked. I asked many questions about what to do about the nuclear plants, but nobody said anything. I quickly understood that Kashiwazaki is like a small town: people don't talk about nuclear power because you might be against nukes, but your neighbor might be working for the power company. Remaining silent is a tactic to keep the peace.
>
> So I changed the topic, and I organized a conversation where the topic was not nukes but the future of the city: in fifty years, what kind of Kashiwazaki do you want to see? Everyone shared their thinking, and they found, to their surprise, that the future they want to create is the same for both groups: a city to which their offspring can come back with pride. The people who are pro-nuke think that they need to have nuclear power to create the economic activity necessary for this, and the people who are against think that theirs is the way

to create such a future. So they found that they have the same goal, but different ways to reach it. This changed the whole atmosphere, and they started to talk, and we ended the three-year project with a good result.

The members of this group were all born in the city of Kashiwazaki, so they talked about their origins: when they were young what kind town it had been and what kind of noises and smells they had enjoyed. When you tap into such a common root, you can find common stories or history or culture, which can become a basis for conversation.

Organizations and local communities have many problems, but I think these boil down to problems in relationships. When I was in graduate school, my major was psychology, and I did some counseling at the university. I found that when people forget or lose important connections with themselves, mental problems will emerge. When I moved into the environmental field, I discovered that the problem is the same: when people lose their connection with the Earth, environmental problems will emerge. And when I started to engage in community building, I found the same: when people lose their connection with their history or culture or inspiration, community problems will emerge.

So what I have been doing in my life is to try to help people rediscover and restore important connections.

To be able to relate effectively with others as (1) fellow actors and (2) fellow parties, we must also relate with them as (3) fellow kin, through rediscovering and restoring the deeper connections among us. Put another way: recognizing and committing to our relationships enables us to (1) solve common problems and (2) negotiate. Although many of us are able to do this within our immediate family or community, to transform our organizations and societies we need to stretch to also do this with people who are more distant from us.

Collaborating with unlike others involves harnessing three universal human drives that undergird these three ways of relating and that are in permanent tension: love (the drive to reconnection), power (the drive to self-realization), and justice (the drive to right relationship).[9] This is the tension King was referring to in the speech I quoted earlier, in which he went on to say: "Power at its best is love implementing the demands of justice, and justice at its best is power correcting everything that stands against love."[10]

The sixth everyday habit of radical engagement, collaborating with unlike others to transform systems, works with love, power, and justice to make our differences productive and generative.

AN EVERYDAY PRACTICE FOR COLLABORATING WITH UNLIKE OTHERS

Here is a way to practice Habit 6: a particular Do step in the general Plan-Do-Study-Act cycle described at the end of chapter 1.

1. Engage with another person in the system who has capacities that are complementary to yours. (That person might also be very different from you, even an opponent.)

2. Through this engagement, develop a hypothesis about how, if the two of you could work through your differences, you would be able to accomplish more together than you would separately.

3. Stretch to take one small new action together.

PERSEVERING
AND RESTING

As I've noted throughout this book, a system is organized and structured, often over many years, in a way that produces and reproduces its characteristic set of behaviors. It can be reorganized and restructured to produce different behaviors, but rarely easily or quickly. System transformation is therefore a long and winding journey—not a short or straightforward project. Radical engagement involves adjusting our pace and course as we go—not just sprinting for a short while, nor just pushing on until we burn out. We combine persevering and resting to ensure that we remain effective and healthy on the journey.

SYSTEMS TRANSFORMATION IS A LONG JOURNEY

Phillip Atiba Solomon is the chair and Carl I. Hovland Professor of African American Studies and professor of psychology at Yale University, and the principal at JusticeRx, a production company with a deal at CBS Studios. He is also the cofounder and CEO of the Center for Policing Equity (CPE), which measures bias in policing in order to stop it. One in five Americans interacts with law enforcement yearly; of those encounters, one million result in the use of force, and Black people are two to four times more likely to have force used against them than are White people. CPE works with police to measure behaviors and revise policies so that fewer people are killed and jailed. Solomon is in it for the long haul.

I asked Solomon why he has taken on this big nonprofit job in addition to his big academic and media ones, and he answered that he sees it as his responsibility toward the system.

> I've never lost faith that this is the thread in the sweater that you can pull and unravel the most. It seems to me that whenever the state is doing something sinister, it always needs the threat of physical coercion to get that done—and that's morally incomprehensible to vulnerable people. And if you can't regulate that threat of physical coercion, then you're not really operating in a democracy: you're operating with democratic rule under the threat of autocracy or fascism. This is the problem that is scariest and most painful to me and the people who look like me.
>
> I was never doing this work for fun: it was always what needs doing.

Solomon explained that CPE fights for justice by searching for cracks in the public safety system where action can be taken to transform that system. But often these cracks are not where people think they are, and are not yet ready to be worked.

> There's racism, and it works through systems and not just individuals. But it's not obvious where the system

change is going to come from. Is it going to be through getting more diverse chiefs? When I started doing this work, there were no more than four Black police chiefs of major cities, and now the majority of these chiefs are Black, but the problem has continued. Is it going to be through diversifying the police departments? There's some good evidence that that's going to help, but not evidence that that's going to be the right way to go: it's a really huge lift, because convincing Black people that it's a good idea to be the people who go into their own community and kill is a hard sell.

Most of our job is to get wins that can scale the next time everybody cares. You don't get scalable wins in the policing space until there's a major outcry at a protest. And so the job is to get ready for that.

He told me that CPE does its work by engaging systematically with five sets of people whom he described as players in a complicated board game.

Watch the board! At CPE we talk about five external audiences: communities and their leaders, particularly in Black communities; law enforcement and their leaders; elected leaders at the local level, and also state and federal levels; donors; and the science community. The board is all five and where they're moving and how they're thinking about our stuff.

Pay attention to the things that the people we need to do our work need to do their work. And don't be thinking about where people are today; think about where they're going to be in six or twelve or eighteen months: look around the corner where things are about to be, so that you understand how we have to act given how the world is about to move.

He emphasized how large and difficult and long the process is to transform such deeply rooted systems.

So you just try and figure out the right way to do this work, and you hope that if you don't make any meaningful change in your lifetime, then someone will pick up your work in a generation or two or three and say, here are seeds of something really useful. Almost everyone I know is unwilling to let things stay the same, but is willing to live a life where they don't see the change that they're working toward.

You are going to need to understand the size and the scope of this thing you're trying to lift, because otherwise you're just going to burn your back out. This is an ages-long process: anti-Blackness in the United States is a special case of powerful people putting the burdens disproportionately on vulnerable communities, which has been a problem since people started getting together and living in groups. If you don't understand that that is fundamentally undergirding the thing that you're trying to do, then you're going to burn yourself out trying to boil the ocean.

So patience is more important than persistence. Patience allows for you to have a life. Part of my thinking is that I saw a lot of folks in my parents' generation who were really inspiring to me, but what they chose to do with their lives was not inspiring. I didn't want to have a life that looked like theirs, with shattered families and suicide attempts and heart attacks at age fifty. That didn't make sense: it wasn't sustainable. I look at people of my generation, and I'm starting to see them burn all the way out. So part of the work is allowing the people who are doing it to have lives that don't suck.

When you understand the scope and the time frame of this work, you understand that your work has to also be helping other people set up a sustainable life, and to do this yourself.

Solomon's point about the time it really takes to transform systems was echoed by one of his colleagues, Michel Gelobter, executive director of the Yale Center for Environmental Justice. Gelobter has been an energetic and determined systems transformer since he was five years old, when he helped his parents register voters in New York City, and over the six decades since has held leadership positions in business, nonprofit, academic, government, and start-up organizations. He has a lifelong commitment to transformation and knows that doing this takes time—often more than one lifetime. He told me,

I'm trying to increase social justice in the world. I'm not looking for a final solution, a utopia: I'm looking to reduce suffering, increase happiness, rebalance some injustices. I knew pretty young that there was no perfect state I was headed toward: there's hunger in the world, there probably will always be hunger, but the more people who work on hunger, the less hunger there will be.

I think a great model for organizers is the biblical figure of Moses, who led the Israelites for forty years in the wilderness, but died before they entered the Promised Land: somebody who is always trying to do something and doesn't quite get there. That's just the nature of the work.

The nature of the work of transforming systems is that it's never straightforward or easy or quick. If we don't understand that this is the nature of the work, then we will fail.

THE IMPERATIVE OF SYSTEMS TRANSFORMATION

For many people, like me, for whom many systems are working fine, working on systems transformation might seem to be a political, professional, or philosophical option: something we can choose to do. But for others, including racialized people such as Solomon and Gelobter, for whom many systems are working terribly—systems that were built not for but against people like them—transformation is urgent and obligatory.

Engaging with people in such positions, as Fyodor Ovchinnikov told me, enables us to grasp that these systems are "really crying out for transformation—not just like, hmm, maybe I should transform something because that's what I like to do." Acting to transform the terribly working systems of which we are part is, as Marcia Anderson emphasized, not so much an option as a responsibility. It is a moral and ethical obligation; more than that, a matter of life and death.

ADVANCING URGENTLY AND PATIENTLY

Systems transformation involves working with time in contradictory ways: with urgency and patience, with beginning and ending, with pressing on and relaxing.

The first systems transformation effort that I helped set up (rather than only facilitating) was the Sustainable Food Lab, an initiative to make global food supply chains more environmentally and socially sustainable. In 2006, after organizing and facilitating an ambitious series of workshops over two years, I told my colleagues that I thought the hard work was over, so I could now step back and turn my attention to other projects. Social entrepreneur Alison Sander, who had more experience than I with such initiatives, looked at me with incredulity: "Clearly you have no idea what this work requires!"

And she was correct. Workshops and projects can contribute to transforming systems, but only as part of a longer and more complex journey. My role in setting up the Lab was over, but the work of the Lab wasn't, and twenty years later that work is still continuing, now being led by a second generation of staff and participants. We need to keep discerning and deciding what, in any given transformation initiative, our roles and responsibilities are—with a realistic sense of the nature of the work.

Transforming systems requires acting with an eye both to short-term and long-term results. This is the point Haggerty made to me when she said, "It is not credible for leaders to say, 'We're building a system to get out of this mess once and for all' without having a plan to deal with the crisis in front of them." And in my interview of Figueres, she said,

> The most difficult thing for me is that every day I have to balance my impatience, because I know that we have to move much faster than we are, with my patience, because I know that social, political, and economic transformations take time. My greatest challenge is balancing patience and impatience, because I'm 100 percent of both.

Writer Rebecca Solnit has a perspective on perseverance in climate work that comes from having studied other historical examples of systems transformation.

> Someone at the dinner table wanted to know what everyone's turning point on climate was, which is to say she wanted us to tell a story with a pivotal moment. She wanted sudden; all I had was slow, the story of a journey with many steps, gradual shifts, accumulating knowledge, concern, and commitment. A lot had happened but it had happened in many increments over a few decades, not via one transformative anything.
>
> Describing the slowness of change is often confused with acceptance of the status quo. It's really the opposite: an argument that the status quo must be changed, and it will take steadfast commitment to see the job through. It's not accepting defeat; it's accepting the terms of possible victory. Distance runners pace themselves; activists and movements often need to do the same, and to learn from the timelines of earlier campaigns to change the world that have succeeded.[1]

Transforming systems, engaging radically, and working with the six everyday habits described so far all require this seventh one: persevering. By persevering through the ups and downs and advances and retreats of this journey, we learn and become more able to contribute. With hindsight I can see that my persevering with this work over the last thirty years has gradually enabled me, through much trial and much error, to better understand and enact these habits—and especially to emphasize particular, small, humble, patient, emergent, direct engagements with diverse others.

STRATEGIC REST

Acting impatiently and patiently, urgently and for a long time, also demands doing the opposite: resting. In my interview with Solomon, he referred to setting up "a sustainable life," and he walked this talk when he took months to reply to my request for a meeting because he was prioritizing his paternity leave. The work of transforming systems requires taking time away from this work to look after ourselves and others.

A healthy movement toward a healthy future requires healthy people. The way we show up affects what we can do. We won't be able to engage radically (below the surface) if we don't take care of ourselves and our companions and kin; the journey is long and hard, and we must acknowledge the uphill. Many of our fellow journeyers, especially those with less power and privilege, are suffering, traumatized, and frightened, torn between resignation and rage. Radical engagement must be empathetic and fair, recognizing that different people face different realities and have different resources and constraints.

Gelobter introduced me to Tamara Toles O'Laughlin, a long-time environmental activist and the founder of Climate Critical, a feminist, antiracist environmental organization dedicated to normalizing a culture that centers care and repair. "If we're going to keep making ambitious claims and mobilizing and having massive strategies and big campaigns," she says, "we need to have people who are rested and able to do it or have enough space to have creative ideas about solving problems. What we don't have is that kind of ethic for the work itself, so people burn out—and they leave."[2]

In writing my books, I have also experienced the value of alternating persevering and resting. Writing requires, above all else, persevering: coming up with an idea, writing it down,

Persevering and resting

reading it, getting feedback from others, and then rewriting, and doing this a hundred times. And when I don't know what to write next, I step away from my desk—have a run or a drive or a sleep—and almost always, through relaxing, I come up with a useful next idea. I advance by alternating between working and not working—like Canada geese, which migrate over long distances, navigating to their destination with rest stops along the way, flying in a V shape and rotating out of the lead position to conserve their energy.

One reason so many of my stories of system transformation breakthroughs are from multiday residential workshops is that this format enables a group of people, even a group that are in conflict, to relax enough to be able to relate in all three dimensions (Habit 2), see what they are not seeing (Habit 3), notice and work with cracks (Habit 4), experiment with new ideas and actions (Habit 5), and collaborate (Habit 6), and hence to discover how to act more responsibly (Habit 1) and over the long haul (Habit 7).

Early on in South Africa's tumultuous transition, I facilitated a workshop for the cabinet of the Province of Gauteng during which the minister of education spent a whole afternoon sleeping on a sofa in the meeting room. I knew that whatever the value of the workshop itself, I had provided value to the province by enabling this hardworking public servant to rest.

I used to teach a course in systems transformation at the Authentic Leadership in Action summer school in Halifax. The students were enthusiastic and sincere, and sometimes asked me what daily practices enabled me to do what I do. I didn't know how to answer this question because I didn't have a regular practice like meditation, so I used to reply flippantly, "I try to get a good night's sleep and to keep my bowels moving regularly." This answer always disappointed my questioners, who were hoping for a more elevated reply.

Looking back at this, though, I think that my answer contained a vital message: for a person to be able to contribute to system transformation, the basic practice required is to remain rested, stable, and healthy. When I have forgotten this and become stressed and exhausted, on the edge of burning out, I have been unable to maintain the equanimity and openness required to engage radically, and have been grievously less effective.

Progress requires perseverance, but if we just keep pushing ourselves and pushing others, we will produce burnout and breakdown. As important as to-do lists are *not*-to-do lists. Inattention to ourselves—forgetting about ourselves, or identifying ourselves only with our work—creates defensiveness and rigidity. Self-awareness, humility, and generosity are required for openness and creativity and therefore for impact. We need to take time for rest, refreshment, reconnection, relaxation, reflection, recovery, and renewal, and to celebrate our victories and honor our losses.

LEARNING TO LIVE TOGETHER

Figueres once invited me to participate in a retreat for climate activists at Plum Village, the monastic community in southwest France founded by her Buddhist teacher, Thich Nhat Hanh. The center told us that accommodation would be in simple shared rooms, but I like having my own private space and so arrived worrying about this arrangement. When I got to my room, however, I found a pamphlet on the desk, titled "Practicing to Live in Harmony in a Shared Space," which contained the following sentences that seemed to be written just for me: "To live amongst each other, . . . we should learn to practice these two wonderful things: compassionate listening and the language of loving speech. An act of compassion always brings about transformation." Transforming systems so that we can live harmoniously in a space we are sharing with others—a room, a community, Earth—requires engaging radically, including through listening compassionately and speaking lovingly. And my biggest learning from the Plum Village monastics came not from their lectures or facilitation but from listening to one of them describe their quarrels in the communal kitchen over the right way to chop vegetables. Radical engagement is, as Manuel first described it to me, the ordinary, everyday, simple-but-not-easy practice of listening and speaking to work out how to live together with connection, agency, and justice.

While I was finishing the writing of this book, I went to New York City for a weekend to hang out with Gelobter. In my interview with him a few months before, he had emphasized that like Moses we might not see systems transformation toward environmental justice within our lifetime, and now he was organizing a conference on "Environmental Joy."

> Joy is a transformative force with diverse meanings. It can be innate, born of grace when one feels in harmony with nature, community, faith, culture, laws and policy, or even the economy. It is what injustice can take from us and what we regain when healing and repair occur. Joy is a core piece of what we seek when working for justice. It is celebrated in community and can also be an expression of the goal that sustains the work for a better world.[3]

I asked him about the connection between systems transformation and joy, and he answered,

> I get a lot of joy out of seeing how people survive and thrive in the face of adversity: it's a source of wonderment

and is very sustaining. There are a lot of lessons to be learned there: rather than only looking at people who are oppressed or in trouble as needing to be defended, there's also generative work grounded in the wisdom and resilience of people who are on the front lines and already facing the horrible things that maybe the rest of us will be facing soon, and understanding how they do well. I don't focus only on the problems, but also on the joy that we will experience when we get rid of these problems. And there's finding joy in the everyday work and the people you work with and how you work with them.

The seventh everyday habit of radical engagement, persevering and resting, involves stretching to pace ourselves, like distance runners, for the long journey of systems transformation. James Baldwin said, "A journey is called that because you cannot know what you will discover on the journey, what you will do with what you find, or what you find will do to you."[4] We stretch not only toward the joy of a transformed system (which will probably not turn out as we dream of, nor happen in our lifetimes) but also toward enjoying the everyday experiences of journeying—companions, battles, advances, defeats, discovery, bewilderment, wonder, discovery, learning—and what these do to us.

AN EVERYDAY PRACTICE FOR PERSEVERING AND RESTING

Here is a way to practice Habit 7: a particular Do step in the general Plan-Do-Study-Act cycle described at the end of chapter 1.

1. Engage with another person in the system who is also on a journey to transform it.

2. Share your experiences of persevering and of resting.

3. Stretch to take one small action to increase your health and effectiveness on the journey.

BEGIN ANYWHERE

This book offers an answer to the question I started asking three years ago: How can all of us, whatever our positions and powers, contribute to transforming the systems we are part of, toward greater connection, agency, and justice?

The answer I have arrived at, by engaging with many outstanding systems transformation practitioners, is this: we contribute through radical engagement, the day-in, day-out practice of intentionally and consciously connecting, colliding, communicating, confronting, competing, and collaborating with people from different parts and levels of the system. The seven everyday habits for transforming systems explained in the previous seven chapters are different facets of this powerfully catalytic way of being, relating, and acting. Radical engagement is effective and exhilarating—but not easy.

As I have pointed out throughout this book, transforming systems is never easy or straightforward. There is no recipe for what you must do: the seven habits are ingredients that you

Begin anywhere

employ in accordance with the particularities of the system you are working with and of your position in it. Radical engagement is a way to discover, in your particular situation, what you can and must do next.

So how can you start to engage radically or to take your engagement to the next level? Not by waiting until you are certain of the right place or way to start. "There's a temptation," avant-garde composer John Cage said, "to do nothing simply because there's so much to do that one doesn't know where to begin. Begin anywhere."[1]

To contribute to transforming a system that you are part of and care about, "Begin anywhere" means: take a step beyond your habitual, familiar, comfortable position toward one where you sense an opportunity, while engaging with other people (preferably people with whom you don't usually engage), attentively and energetically. Taking this single, small, simple-but-not-easy step will lead you to a next one and then one after that—like a baby deer, standing up, alertly looking around, taking baby steps, and thereby learning how to get around and deal with its context.

When I facilitate workshops of people collaborating to transform a system, one surprisingly productive activity is for the group to use Lego bricks to coconstruct a physical model of the system or of some other aspect of their work. And in using this structured innovation method, a surprisingly productive ground rule is, "If you don't know what to build, just start building."[2] The act of working with your hands generates a way forward that you didn't previously have in mind. Radical engagement works the same way: the act of engaging with others generates a way forward that you didn't previously have in mind. Just start engaging.

The seven habits of radical engagement offer seven possible ways to begin:

1. Acting Responsibly: engage to clarify your own role and responsibility
2. Relating in Three Dimensions: engage with emphasis on the dimension(s) that you've been neglecting
3. Looking for What's Unseen: engage to enrich your understanding of what's happening
4. Working with Cracks: engage to move toward, into, and through openings that are arising
5. Experimenting a Way Forward: engage to systematically try out new possibilities
6. Collaborating with Unlike Others: engage to advance better together
7. Persevering and Resting: engage to participate fully and joyfully for the long haul

Begin anywhere and go everywhere. There is no road map for transforming systems and no one right or best place to start. You can't know what will work, so you must simply start somewhere that you think presents an opening. Screw up your courage to take a step forward, however small, and then see where you are and what your next step will be.

Whichever habit you start with, all of them fit together and enable each other. As you learn to see what you are not seeing, for example, you become more able to see cracks, and opportunities to work with them; as you learn to relate in all three dimensions, you become more able to connect and collaborate with unlike others; as you persevere and rest, you develop the stamina and relaxation that enables you to experiment a way forward.

By engaging in these ways, we learn and grow and become more able to live active, connected, grounded, healthy, joyful lives. And we become more able to contribute to creating a better world. Let's do this.

EVERYDAY HABITS FOR TRANSFORMING SYSTEMS DISCUSSION GUIDE

This book describes a powerful, catalytic way of being, relating, and acting—radical engagement—that enables us to contribute to transforming systems. Radical engagement involves attending to the particularities of the system we want to transform and of our position in it. The purpose of this discussion guide is to help individuals and groups wrestle with applying radical engagement in their particular situations.

PREFACE

What is a system you are part of that you think needs to change fundamentally?

For whom is this system working? For whom is it not working?

Which aspects of this system do you think need to be preserved and which need to be transformed?

What aspects of this system do you think you need not or cannot contribute to transforming? What aspects of the system do you think you need to and can contribute to transforming?

What doubts and hopes do you have about the contribution you can make?

INTRODUCTION

What lessons do you take away from the stories of Trevor Manuel and the South African transition?

What thoughts and feelings does the drawing of the savanna evoke for you?

What have you learned from your experiences of how systems are and are not transformed?

What images, thoughts, and feelings does the term *cracks* evoke for you?

What images, thoughts, and feelings does the term *radical engagement* evoke for you?

What images, thoughts, and feelings do the briefly described seven habits of radical engagement evoke for you?

HABIT 1

What lessons, about this and other habits, do you take away from the stories of Marcia Anderson and the Manitoba First Nations health project?

What thoughts and feelings does the drawing of the elephants evoke for you?

What particular system are you concerned about, and what role are you playing in it?

What responsibilities does this role imply?

What can and must you do?

What practices do you employ for acting responsibly?

HABIT 2

What lessons, about this and other habits, do you take away from the stories of Christiana Figueres's work leading up to COP 15 and of Adam Kahane at COP 27?

How does Donella Meadows's understanding of systems relate to yours?

What thoughts and feelings does the drawing of the wolves evoke for you?

Of the three dimensions of relating with others (as fellow actors, as fellow parties, as fellow kin), which do you default to and employ most? Which do you shy away from and employ least?

What practices do you employ to strengthen your weaker dimension(s) and to relate in all three dimensions?

HABIT 3

What lessons, about this and other habits, do you take away from the stories of Juan Manuel Santos, Francisco de Roux, and the Destino Colombia project?

What thoughts and feelings does the drawing of the stick insect evoke for you?

What do you tend not to see? What do you think is obstructing your seeing?

What practices do you employ for looking for what you are not seeing?

HABIT 4

What lessons, about this and other habits, do you take away from Al Etmanski's story?

How does Frances Westley's theory of systems transformation relate to your own experiences?

What thoughts and feelings does the drawing of the plants and roots evoke for you?

What cracks are you sensing in the systems you are part of?

Do you tend to shy away from or move toward cracks? Do you paper over or work with them?

What practices do you employ for working with cracks?

HABIT 5

What lessons, about this and other habits, do you take away from the stories of Sumit Champrasit, Jane Davidson, and the US-China dialogue project?

What thoughts and feelings does the drawing of the octopus evoke for you?

What have you learned from your experiences with trial and error?

Do you tend to shy away from or embrace experimentation and learning by doing?

What practices do you employ for experimenting a way forward?

HABIT 6

What lessons, about this and other habits, do you take away from the stories of Rosanne Haggerty, Ishmael Mkhabela, and Junko Edahiro?

What thoughts and feelings does the drawing of the plover and the crocodile evoke for you?

What have you learned from your experience with collaborating with unlike others?

Do you tend to shy away from or embrace collaborating with unlike others?

What practices do you employ for making differences productive and for collaborating with unlike others?

HABIT 7

What lessons, about this and other habits, do you take away
from the stories of Phillip Atiba Solomon, Michel Gelobter,
and Tamara Toles O'Laughlin?

What thoughts and feelings does the drawing of the geese evoke
for you?

Do you tend to sprint only for a short while (not persevere) and/
or push on until you burn out (not rest)?

What practices do you employ for synergizing patience and
impatience?

What practices do you employ for synergizing persevering and
resting?

CONCLUSION

What thoughts and feelings does the drawing of the fawn evoke
for you?

What everyday actions do you want to practice to strengthen
your capacity to engage radically?

What everyday actions will you now start doing, stop doing, and
keep doing?

NOTES

INTRODUCTION

1   See Adam Kahane, "Facilitating Breakthrough on Equality: Adam Kahane in Conversation with Trevor Manuel," "Facilitating Breakthrough on Climate: Adam Kahane in Conversation with Christiana Figueres," and "Facilitating Breakthrough on Peace: Adam Kahane in Conversation with President Santos," October 2021, https://www.reospartners.com.

2   Cited in Isaiah Berlin, *The Crooked Timber of Humanity: Chapters in the History of Ideas* (Princeton, NJ: Princeton University Press, 2013), ix.

3   Alex Perry, "Trevor Manuel: The Veteran." *Time*, March 25, 2009, https://time.com/archive/6688002/trevor-manuel-the-veteran/.

4   See Adam Kahane, *Transformative Scenario Planning: Working Together to Change the Future* (Oakland, CA: Berrett-Koehler, 2012), 1–13.

5   Unpublished interview notes for Glennifer Gillespie and Elena Díez Pinto, "The Footprints of Mont Fleur: The Mont Fleur Scenario Project, South Africa, 1991–1992," in *Learning Histories: Democratic Dialogue Regional Project*, ed. Katrin Käufer (New York: United Nations Development Programme Regional Bureau for Latin America and the Caribbean, 2004).

6   Gillespie and Pinto.

7   Naomi Klein, *Doppelganger: A Trip into the Mirror World* (New York: Knopf, 2023), 342.

8   *The Concise Oxford Dictionary of Current English*, 7th ed. (1983), s.v. "engage," "engagement," and "radical."

HABIT 1

1   See Melanie MacKinnon and Adam Kahane, "Braiding Indigenous and Settler Methodologies: Learnings from a First Nations Health Transformation Project in Manitoba," December 13, 2019, https://reospartners.com/braiding-indigenous-and-settler-methodologies-learnings-from-a-first-nations-health-transformation-project-in-manitoba/.

2   Audre Lorde, "The Master's Tools Will Never Dismantle the Master's House," in *Sister Outsider: Essays and Speeches* (Berkeley, CA: Crossing Press, 2007), 110–114.

3   Thomas King, *All My Relations: An Anthology of Contemporary Canadian Native Prose* (Toronto: McClelland & Stewart, 1990), ix.

4   Odette Auger, "Decolonial Futures: Climate Education That Faces Complexity, Denial, and Discomfort," *Watershed Sentinel*, May 12, 2023, https://watershedsentinel.ca/articles/climate-education-and-reotti/.

5   See Philip Mirvis and Karen Ayas, *To the Desert and Back: The Story of One of the Most Dramatic Business Transformations on Record* (Hoboken, NJ: Jossey-Bass), 2007.

6   *Oxford Essential Quotations*, 4th ed. (2016).

7   Patty Krawek, *Becoming Kin: An Indigenous Call to Unforgetting the Past and Reimagining Our Future* (Minneapolis, MN: Broadleaf Books, 2002), 3.

8   Ronald Moen and Clifford Norman, "Circling Back: Clearing Up Myths about the Deming Cycle and Seeing How It Keeps Evolving," November 2010, http://www.apiweb.org/circling-back.pdf.

HABIT 2

1   Donella Meadows, *Thinking in Systems: A Primer* (White River Junction, VT: Chelsea Green Publishing, 2008), 188.

2 Meadows, 11.

3 Meadows, 16.

4 Leslie Proctor, "Editor's Notebook: A Quotation with a Life of Its Own," *Patient Safety & Quality Healthcare*, July 1, 2008, https://www.psqh.com/analysis/editor-s-notebook-a-quotation-with-a-life-of-its-own/.

5 Ninawa Huni Kui and Vanessa Andreotti, "Views from COP 27: How the Climate Conference Could Confront Colonialism by Centring Indigenous Rights," *The Conversation*, November 9, 2022, https://theconversation.com/views-from-cop27-how-the-climate-conference-could-confront-colonialism-by-centring-indigenous-rights-194223.

6 Michele-Lee Moore, Darcy Riddell, and Dana Vocisano, "Scaling Out, Scaling Up, Scaling Deep: Strategies of Non-Profits in Advancing Systemic Social Innovation," *Journal of Corporate Citizenship*, no. 58 (June 2015), 67–84, http://www.jstor.org/stable/jcorpciti.58.67.

7 Johann Wolfgang von Goethe, *Scientific Studies* (New York: Suhrkamp Publishers, 1988), 39.

HABIT 3

1 Adam Kahane, *Collaborating with the Enemy: How to Work with People You Don't Agree With or Like or Trust* (Oakland, CA: Berrett-Koehler, 2017), 41–46.

2 "The Nobel Peace Prize 2016," press release, October 7, 2016, https://www.nobelprize.org/prizes/peace/2016/press-release.

3 Juan Manuel Santos, "Siempre en búsqueda de la paz" ["Always Searching for Peace"], press release, October 7, 2016, https://es.presidencia.gov.co.

4 James Baldwin, "As Much Truth as One Can Bear," *New York Times*, January 14, 1962, https://www.nytimes.com/1962/01/14/archives/as-much-truth-as-one-can-bear-to-speak-out-about-the-world-as-it-is.html.

5 Juan Manuel Santos, "Palabras del Presidente Juan Manuel Santos en la presentación del libro 'El poder y el amor' de Adam Kahane."

[Remarks of President Juan Manuel Santos at the presentation of the book *Power and Love* by Adam Kahane]" (Bogotá, Colombia, February 21, 2012).

6   William Ury, *Possible: How We Survive (and Thrive) in an Age of Conflict* (New York: Harper Business, 2024), back cover.

7   Adam Kahane, *Facilitating Breakthrough: How to Remove Obstacles, Bridge Differences, and Move Forward Together* (Oakland, CA: Berrett-Koehler, 2021), 1–4.

8   Angela Wilkinson and Roland Kupers, *The Essence of Scenarios: Learning from the Shell Experience* (Amsterdam: Amsterdam University Press, 2014).

9   Art Kleiner, "The Man Who Saw the Future," *strategy+business*, February 12, 2003, https://www.strategy-business.com/article/8220.

10 Unpublished interview notes for Glennifer Gillespie and Elena Díez Pinto, "The Footprints of Mont Fleur: The Mont Fleur Scenario Project, South Africa, 1991–1992," in *Learning Histories: Democratic Dialogue Regional Project*, ed. Katrin Käufer (New York: United Nations Development Programme Regional Bureau for Latin America and the Caribbean, 2004).

11 Shane Parrish, "How Darwin Thought: The Golden Rule of Thinking," *FS* (blog), accessed August 17, 2024, https://fs.blog/charles -darwin-thinker/.

HABIT 4

1   Al Etmanski, *Impact: Six Patterns to Spread Your Social Innovation* (Prince Edward Island, Canada: Orwell Cove, 2015), 21–22.

2   Adapted from "How Do You Change the System When You Don't Own It, with Frances Westley," *Gary Hamel, The New Human Movement*, video, March 8, 2022, https://www.garyhamel.com/video/how -do-you-change-system-when-you-don%E2%80%99t-own-it-frances -westley.

3   Katharine McGowan, Frances Westley, and Ola Tjörnbo, eds., *The Evolution of Social Innovation: Building Resilience through Transitions* (Cheltenham, England: Edward Elgar Publishing, 2017).

4   Frances Westley, "Conclusion: Recognizing Transformative Potential" in *Evolution of Social Innovation*, ed. McGowan et al.", 254.

5   Frances Westley, "The Social Innovation Dynamic," October 2008, 5, https://www.torontomu.ca/content/dam/cpipe/documents/Why/Frances%20Westley%2C%20Social%20Innovation%20Dynamic.pdf.

6   Frances Westley, Brenda Zimmerman, and Michael Quinn Patton, *Getting to Maybe: How the World Is Changed* (Toronto: Vintage Canada, 2007), 21.

7   Westley et al., 76.

8   Westley et al., 78.

9   Bayo Akomolafe, "What I Mean by Postactivism," *Blog*, November 13, 2020, https://www.bayoakomolafe.net/post/what-i-mean-by-postactivism.

10 Dawn Porter, *John Lewis: Good Trouble* (New York: Magnolia Pictures, 2020), film.

HABIT 5

1   "David Snowden," Cynefin Co, accessed August 17, 2024, https://thecynefin.co/team/dave-snowden/.

2   Chris Corrigan, "A Tour around the Latest Cynefin Iteration," *Parking Lot* (blog), March 23, 2020, https://www.chriscorrigan.com/parkinglot/a-tour-around-the-latest-cynefin-iteration/.

3   Chris Corrigan, "Figure It Out . . . (aka, How to Use the Cynefin Framework)," *Parking Lot* (blog), August 31, 2020, https://www.chriscorrigan.com/parkinglot/figure-it-out/.

4   Chris Corrigan, "Affordances in the Two Loops," *Parking Lot* (blog), January 7, 2024, https://www.chriscorrigan.com/parkinglot/affordances-in-the-two-loops/.

5   "Crossing the River by Touching the Stones," Wikipedia, accessed August 17, 2024, https://en.wikipedia.org/wiki/Crossing_the_river_by_touching_the_stones.

6   Westley et al.; Ury.

7   Henri-Georges Clouzot, *The Mystery of Picasso* (Paris: Filmsonor, 1956), film.

8   John Keats, *The Complete Poetical Works and Letters of John Keats* (Boston: Houghton, Mifflin, 1899), 277.

HABIT 6

1   Community Solutions, "Homelessness Is a Solvable Systems Problem," YouTube, accessed August 17, 2024, https://www.youtube.com /watch?v=tMPTjKDVjTo.

2   *The Concise Oxford Dictionary of Current English*, 7th ed. (1983), s.v. "collaboration."

3   Dharna Noor, "Exclude Fossil Fuel Firms from Cop28 If They Only Want to Obstruct, Says ex-UN Chief," *Guardian,* September 21, 2023, https://www.theguardian.com/environment/2023/sep/21/un -cop28-fossil-fuel-firms-climate-action.

4   Adam Kahane, *Collaborating with the Enemy: How to Work with People You Don't Agree With or Like or Trust* (Oakland, CA: Berrett-Koehler, 2017), 3.

5   James Hillman, *Kinds of Power: A Guide to Its Intelligent Uses* (New York: Doubleday, 1995), 108.

6   Martin Luther King Jr., "Where Do We Go from Here?" in *The Essential Martin Luther King, Jr.,* ed. Clayborne Carson (Boston: Beacon Press, 2013), 220–21.

7   See Adam Kahane, *Power and Love: A Theory and Practice of Social Change* (Oakland, CA: Berrett-Koehler, 2010).

8   Klaus Schwab, *Stakeholder Capitalism: A Global Economy That Works for Progress, People and Planet* (Hoboken, NJ: Wiley, 2021).

9   Adam Kahane, "Radical Collaboration to Transform Social Systems: Moving Forward Together with Love, Power, and Justice." *Journal of Awareness-Based Systems Change* 3, no. 2, 23–40, https://doi.org /10.47061/jasc.v3i2.6709.

10   King, 221.

HABIT 7

1   Rebecca Solnit, "Slow Change Can Be Radical Change," *Literary Hub*, January 11, 2024, https://lithub.com/rebecca-solnit-slow-change-can-be-radical-change/.

2   Yessenia Funes, "The Environmental Movement Faces Burnout. This Woman Wants to Repair That," *Atmos*, August 17, 2022, https://atmos.earth/tamara-toles-o-laughlin-climate-activism-burnout/.

3   Environmental Joy: Roadmaps for Resistance, Resilience, and Thriving [conference], Yale Center for Environmental Justice, accessed August 17, 2024, https://ycej.yale.edu/en/conference-2024.

4   Raoul Peck, *I Am Not Your Negro* (New York: Magnolia Pictures, 2017), film.

CONCLUSION

1   John Cage, *A Year from Monday: New Lectures and Writings* (Middletown, CT: Wesleyan University Press, 1967), 54.

2   Per Kristiansen and Robert Rasmussen, *Building a Better Business Using the Lego Serious Play Method* (Hoboken, NJ: Wiley, 2014).

ACKNOWLEDGMENTS

I advance in my thinking and writing more through engaging in conversation than through reading, and I have written this book, over twelve intense months, by talking with colleagues, friends, and strangers all around the world, on one-on-one and group Zoom calls and in LinkedIn threads, Google Docs, and cafes and living rooms. I am grateful for all of the thoughtful, generous, patient, challenging, committed contributions, including from the following people (with apologies for any inadvertent omissions):

Rosa María Abdelnour, Gonzalo Muñoz Abogabir, Chaitanya Ahuja, Akanimo Akpan, Adam Ambrogi, Marcia Anderson, Sean Andrew, Jan Archer, Clara Arenas, Brenna Atnikov, Michelle Baldwin, Tom Baldwin, Jany Barraut, Elena Battaglini, Veronica Baz, Laleh Behjat, Andrew Bell, Monica Bensberg, Simon Berg, Stefan Bergheim, Jennifer Beyer, Sonja Blignaut, Peter Block, Raimondo Boggia, Mille Bøjer, François Bonnici, Ana Borges, Paul Born, Ivona Boroje, Houda Boulahbel, Chantal Boutin, Graham Boyd, Freya Bradford, Alan Briskin, Tim Brodhead, Sarah Brooks, Tie Franco Brotto, Herman Brouwer, Ingrid Bruynse, Meg Buzzi, Mark Cabaj, Liza Cagua-McAllister, Jhozman Camacho, Brock Carlton, Rumon Carter, Manuel José Carvajal, Colleen Casimira, Bernadette Castilho, Sumit Champrasit, Pintian Chen, Sylvia Cheuy, Diana Chigas, Maureen Clarke,

Elizabeth Clement, Charly Clermont, Chris Corrigan, Marie Harbo Dahle, Stacey Dakin, Melissa Dark, Jane Davidson, Janice Dean, Maria Deckeman, Dennise Demming, Christy Dena, Kateryna Derkach, Adalberto Savinon Diez de Sollano, Tim Draimin, Melanie Dubin, Nikhil Dugal, Newell Eaton, Junko Edahiro, John Elkington, Jayne Engle, Sara Enright, Josh Epperson, Gorka Espiau, Al Etmanski, Ng Yeuk Fan, Fabrizio Faraco, Estrella Fichter, Caroline Figueres, Betty Sue Flowers, Gwynne Foster, Tatiana Fraser, Rebecca Freeth, Steph French, Caitlin Frost, Bill Fulton, Mary Gelinas, Michel Gelobter, Kathryn Gichini, Sarah Gillen, James Gimian, Karen Goldberg, Arielle Goodman, Carol Gorelick, Julia Griss, Rosy Gues, Steve Vinay Gunther, Paul Hackenmueller, Rosanne Haggerty, Hal Hamilton, Karen Hand, Calvin Haney, Eiji Harada, Avner Haramati, Lyn Hartley, Bruce Allen Hecht, Nitzan Hermon, Berend-Jan Hilberts, Hezekiah Holland, Ky Holland, Cole Hoover, Stephen Huddart, Alan Hudson, Christie Huff, Constantine Iliopoulos, Priti Irani, Antonio Iturra, Mike Jackson, Cédric Jamet, Melanie Jamieson, Tejaswinee Jhunjhunwala, Brendon Johnson, Stephen Johnston, Rachel Jones, David Kahane, Kirsten Kainz, Sandra Killick, Linet Kimathi, Kranthi Kiran, Art Kleiner, Liz Koblyk, Oliver Koenig, Ruth Krivoy, Pascal Kruijsifix, Sanatan Kulshrestha, Danny Kushlink, Jenny Kwan, Sean Lafleur, Jean-Noé Landry, Sirikul Nui Laukaikul, Joanne Lauterjung, Dan Leahy, Sophie Legendre, Graham Leicester, Michael Lennon, Tom Lent, Karen Leu, Lindsay Levin, Steven Lichty, Ralf Lippold, Victor Loh, Jessica Long, Johanne Lortie, Bruce Lourie, Colleen Magner, Imène Maharzi, Johanna Mair, Elizabeth Maloba, Lorraine Margherita, Gerardo Marquez, Jim Marsden, Frances Martin, Adrià Garcia i Mateu, Ludwig May, Bill McAllister-Lovatt, Cheryl McKay, Kevin McNamara, Maria Mendez, Agnes Meneses, Diane Meschino, Parand Meysami, Allie Middleton,

Kathleen Milligan, Naoya Mitake, Katrina Mitchell, Henry Mitzberg, Susi Mølgaard, Nicole Monroe, Wendy Morris, Lerato Mpofu, Cher Murphy, Jerry Nagel, Zuzana Navratil, Meret Nehe, Maria Ana Botelho Neves, James Newcomb, Monique Newton, Nicole Ng, Tara Polzer Ngwato, Sibout Nooteboom, Staffan Nöteberg, Riichiro Oda, Jessica Ogden, Seamus O'Gorman, Eric Olson, Hana Alisa Omer, Hernán Hochschild Ovalle, Fyodor Ovchinnikov, Mikael Paltschik, Anna Papadaki, Michelle Parlevliet, Danya Pastuszek, Bhavesh Patel, Sheela Patel, Kat Pattillo, Juan Manuel Cheaz Pelaez, Dave Pendle, Thomas Perret, Gina Phelan, Gregory Phillips, Mark Pickering, Mary Pickering, Steve Piersanti, Peter Plastrik, Monica Pohlmann, Eva Pomeroy, John Poparad, Ana Porzecanski, Bill Potapchuk, Ian Prinsloo, Catalina Puscasu, Tamzin Ractliffe, Daniele Radici, Rooksana Rajab, Michael Randel, Lorraine Randell, Antares Reisky, Manuela Restrepo, Jo Reynolds, Amanda Ripley, Guilherme Rodrigues, Aurelia Roman, Loretta Rose, Taryn Rose, Nancy Rosenfeld, Leon Rosenthal, Francisco de Roux, Alain Ruche, Alex Ryan, Sharon Ryan, Alexander Samarin, Rebecca Sampson, Catherine Sands, Manal Sayid, Doug Schneider, Anita Schröder, Claude Schryer, Valeria Scorza, Jessica Seddon, Cynthia Selin, Khai Seng, Mpinane Senkhane, Conor Seyle, Bill Sharpe, Etrit Shkreli, Yuliya Shtaltovna, Gary Shunk, Jotham Sietsma, Josiane Smith, David Snowden, Hafidha Sofia, Joel Solomon, Phillip Atiba Solomon, Julian Sonn, Melissa Spatz, Brandon Springle, Rhonda St. Croix, Denisa Steiper, Marilyn Struthers, Marwa Suraj, Jacqui Syndercombe, Grant Symons, Cristina Temmink, Anoush Terjanian, Chris Thompson, William Torbert, Aaron Trowbridge, Terrance Turpin, Marco Valente, Maria Vamvalis, Linda Vanderlee, Tom Van den Steen, Henrique Vedana, Andrés Felipe Vera-Ramírez, Dennis Vergne, Emmanuelle Vital, Phil Volkofsky, Steve Waddell, Gabrielle Walker, Fritz Walter, Jon

Walton, Yannick Wassmer, Brandon Wiers, Ian Wight, Angela
Wilkinson, Luan Williams, David Winter, Teresa Woodland,
Larry Yang, Wan-Ching Yang, Joel Yanowitz, Anita Zaenker,
Stephanie Zanettin, Junwei Zhu, and Zuzana Žilkova.

One of the pleasures of this engaging process has been conversations that showed me something crucial that I wasn't seeing
and so caused the book to shift fundamentally. For these illuminating moments I am grateful to the following people (with
apologies again for omissions): Mille Bøjer, for pointing out that
the book needed to center the experiences of my interviewees;
Tim Brodhead, that system transformers are by definition disruptive; Mark Cabaj, that systems transformation is cumulative
rather than a one-off; Rumon Carter, that the preface needed
to be evocative rather than only analytical (inspired in turn by
poet Anis Mojgani); Betty Sue Flowers, that the practices I am
writing about are habits for breaking habits; James Gimian, that
the book's story is of discovery and that capacities are uncovered
more than welded on; Riichiro Oda, that working effectively
with systems requires particular habits; Fyodor Ovchinnikov,
that systems transformation needs to be more than a nice-to-do;
Steve Piersanti, that the key transformational move is engaging; Marco Valente, that there is no recipe for transformation;
Jon Walton, that opening oneself up is risky; Yannick Wassmer,
that systems transformation looks completely different from the
perspective of those whom the system is against; and Siobhan
Wilkinson, that recognizing our position in a system is the foundational habit.

This books builds on an earlier collaborative interviewing
and writing project that produced *Radical Collaboration to Accelerate Climate Action: A Guidebook for Working Together with
Speed, Scale, and Justice*, and I am grateful to that team for their
inspiration: Colleen Casimira, Nikhil Dugal, Ramiro Fernandez,

Betty Sue Flowers, Fabio Issao, Melanie Jamieson, Tejaswinee Jhunjhunwala, Lindsay Levin Sam Mabaso, Joe McCarron, Nicole Ng, Mahmood Sonday, Zoe Tcholak-Antitch, Nigel Topping, and Jon Walton.

I am able to write my books because I have a longstanding partnership with the wonderful team at Berrett-Koehler Publishers. For this book I am grateful for the contributions of Cathy Mallon, Susan Geraghty, Ashley Ingram, Michele Jones, Christy Kirk, Lewelin Polanco, Jessica Siddiqi, Jeevan Sivasubramaniam, the three conscientious reviewers (Maria Lewytzky-Milligan, John Perkins, and Alexandra Stavros), and especially the brilliant, patient, demanding Steven Piersanti.

This book has been, more than my previous ones, a family project. I am grateful for the support and inspiration from Allan Boesak, Pulane Boesak-Zake, Caelin Thyssen, Siobhan Wilkinson, and, above all, my beloved Dorothy.

INDEX

Page numbers followed by *i* refer to an image on that page.

ABOUT THE AUTHOR

For thirty-five years, Adam Kahane has focused passionately on learning how to transform societal systems and on helping others do the same.

Adam is a practical practitioner whose work on solving tough problems is recognized around the world. He cofounded Reos Partners, an international social enterprise that supports teams of government, business, and civil society leaders to collaborate across differences to address their most crucial systemic challenges. He has led teams working toward, among other objectives, democracy in South Africa, peace in Colombia, educational reforms in Mexico, health equity in the US, Indigenous self-determination in Canada, security in Europe, child nutrition in India, and good governance in Thailand, and, at larger scales, drug policy, food sustainability, and climate resilience. This extensive and intensive experience has given him many opportunities for trial and many opportunities for error and hence many opportunities for learning.

In parallel with and grounded in this applied work in particular contexts, Adam has built up a pioneering body of general practice and theory. He has written five best-selling books, which have been translated into more than twenty languages: *Solving Tough Problems* (about which Nelson Mandela said, "This breakthrough book that addresses the central challenge of our time: finding a way to work together to solve the problems we have created"), *Power and Love, Transformative Scenario Planning, Collaborating with the Enemy,* and *Facilitating Breakthrough.* He wrote this sixth book, *Everyday Habits for Transforming Systems,* because he realized that there was something crucial about systems transformation that he didn't understand and needed to: the practices that any of us can employ to contribute to creating a better world.

Adam is a member of the Order of Canada and a Schwab Foundation Thought Leader awardee, and has been a fellow at the International Institute for Applied Systems Analysis, the Paris Institute for Advanced Study, the University of Oxford, and the World Academy of Art and Science.

Adam has a BSc in physics from McGill University; an MA in energy and resource from the University of California, Berkeley; and an MA in applied behavioral science from Bastyr University. He has also studied negotiation at Harvard Law School and cello performance at Institut Marguerite-Bourgeoys.

Adam and his wife, Dorothy, live in Montreal and Cape Town among four children, ten grandchildren, and a cat named Gata.

adamkahane.com

ABOUT THE ARTIST

Siobhan Wilkinson, known professionally as Club Cliché, is a Montreal-based South African artist specializing in tattoo, painting, and digital art.

Siobhan has a background in social sciences and community engagement and leans into life and the pursuit of anticolonial practices. Her work centers on reclamation and liberation of body and land and explores themes of social transformation and justice. This perspective informs her endeavors as an activist, farmer, and artist.

Instagram @clubcliche

ABOUT REOS PARTNERS

*How Can We Work Together to Solve the Problems
We Have Created?*

Reos Partners is an international social impact company special-
ized in enabling transformative collaboration, even in situations
of high complexity, uncertainty, and polarization.

Our purpose is to support sustainable and equitable progress on humanity's most crucial challenges. Our contribution
to this massive endeavor is to offer a proven approach toward
ensuring that institutional and societal collaboration is effective
when and where it matters most.

We have been facilitating systemic change efforts for more
than twenty years in over eighty countries. We have worked
with agents of change across civil society organizations, governments, foundations, intergovernmental agencies, and corporations, supporting them to work together to shift perspectives
and influence the root causes of societal challenges.

We partner with leaders and leading institutions that are
committed to taking effective and inclusive collaboration to
new levels. We cocreate with our partners and customize our
response based on a deep inquiry into each unique situation.

Our approach works at three levels:

- We build skills, understandings, and capabilities for individuals, teams, and institutions to collaborate both internally and externally.
- We work with teams, organizations, and communities to deliver and embed impactful outcomes and initiatives collaboratively.
- We design and deliver large-scale multi-stakeholder initiatives and alliances to address complex problems and to develop, apply, and institutionalize transformative solutions.

Our globally distributed team is located in fifteen countries on four continents. We pride ourselves on our differences because we know that our strength lies in the diversity of our collective experience. We value humble courage, adaptive rigor, and radical collaboration.

reospartners.com

Berrett–Koehler
Publishers

Berrett-Koehler is an independent publisher dedicated to an ambitious mission: *Connecting people and ideas to create a world that works for all.*

Our publications span many formats, including print, digital, audio, and video. We also offer online resources, training, and gatherings. And we will continue expanding our products and services to advance our mission.

We believe that the solutions to the world's problems will come from all of us, working at all levels: in our society, in our organizations, and in our own lives. Our publications and resources offer pathways to creating a more just, equitable, and sustainable society. They help people make their organizations more humane, democratic, diverse, and effective (and we don't think there's any contradiction there). And they guide people in creating positive change in their own lives and aligning their personal practices with their aspirations for a better world.

And we strive to practice what we preach through what we call "The BK Way." At the core of this approach is *stewardship,* a deep sense of responsibility to administer the company for the benefit of all of our stakeholder groups, including authors, customers, employees, investors, service providers, sales partners, and the communities and environment around us. Everything we do is built around stewardship and our other core values of *quality, partnership, inclusion,* and *sustainability.*

This is why Berrett-Koehler is the first book publishing company to be both a B Corporation (a rigorous certification) and a benefit corporation (a for-profit legal status), which together require us to adhere to the highest standards for corporate, social, and environmental performance. And it is why we have instituted many pioneering practices (which you can learn about at www.bkconnection.com), including the Berrett-Koehler Constitution, the Bill of Rights and Responsibilities for BK Authors, and our unique Author Days.

We are grateful to our readers, authors, and other friends who are supporting our mission. We ask you to share with us examples of how BK publications and resources are making a difference in your lives, organizations, and communities at www.bkconnection.com/impact.

Dear reader,

Thank you for picking up this book and welcome to the worldwide BK community! You're joining a special group of people who have come together to create positive change in their lives, organizations, and communities.

What's BK all about?

Our mission is to connect people and ideas to create a world that works for all.

Why? Our communities, organizations, and lives get bogged down by old paradigms of self-interest, exclusion, hierarchy, and privilege. But we believe that can change. That's why we seek the leading experts on these challenges—and share their actionable ideas with you.

A welcome gift

To help you get started, we'd like to offer you a **free copy** of one of our bestselling ebooks:

www.bkconnection.com/welcome

When you claim your **free ebook**, you'll also be subscribed to our blog.

Our freshest insights

Access the best new tools and ideas for leaders at all levels on our blog at ideas.bkconnection.com.

Sincerely,

Your friends at Berrett-Koehler